The iPad Piano Studio
Keys to Unlocking the Power of Apps

LEILA J VISS

ebGINES
BLISHING

The iPad Piano Studio: Keys to Unlocking the Power of Apps by Leila Viss

Copyright © 2013 by Webgines Publishing – a division of Webgines Communication Inc.

ISBN 978-0-9900010-0-3

Library of Congress Cataloging-in-Publication Data is on file and available upon request.

TRADEMARKS

WARNING AND DISCLAIMER

DISTRIBUTION & BULK SALES

Webgines Publishing offers excellent discounts on this book when ordered in quantity for bulk purchases or special sales events. For more information, please visit www.ipadpianostudio.com or email us at sales@ipadpianostudio.com

Webgines Publishing

A Division Of Webgines Communication Inc.
7372 Walnut Ave, Suite L
Buena Park, California, 90620
United States Of America

Contact Information

Tom Folenta - President
Tom@webgines,com
1-800-501-6436

First Printing: October 2013
Printed in the United States of America

Author	Managing Editor	Lead Programmer
Leila J Viss	Tom Folenta	Jason Hummel
Editor-in-Chief	**Book Designer**	**Mobile Programmer**
Leila J Viss	Ray Mong	Eric Folenta

VIDEO QR ▶

INTRO

HOW DOES THIS BOOK WORK?

If you've peeked ahead, you'll notice this book features short chapters in a question-answer format. This configuration should help you gather information quickly. As you flip or swipe (if you are reading a digital edition) through the pages you can glance at a question and make a decision to read further or move on. In addition, you will find lists and outlines. These may be interjected with brief SIDE NOTE (♪) sessions strategically placed to cheer you on; take a moment to reflect or take a breather from too much information.

VIDEO QR ▶

An extra special feature of this book is the appearance of QR codes (quick response codes). If you spot one, pull out your smart phone or iPad and scan the code to view associated videos. Requirements: Works with any SmartPhone (iPhone, Android, etc.) that can read QR Codes. QR reader apps are free — simply search your phone's app library for QR readers.

WHY WOULD ONE WRITE A BOOK ABOUT USING THE iPAD FOR TEACHING PIANO?

I've posed that question to myself a number of times. Here are my answers in no certain order:

- I am unashamedly infatuated with the iPad and the variety of apps and learning tools it provides and feel the need to share my "love" with others.
- I've used tech-savvy tools to enhance my teaching since my piano studio opened in 1990. The iPad has revolutionized my lab-assisted instruction.
- Someone told me in no uncertain terms that I should write a book about this topic. So simply stated: I'm a pushover.

WHO WOULD WRITE SUCH A BOOK?

I'm best described as one who:

- Has been smitten by the iPad
- Integrates the iPad into just about every lesson
- Can't stop writing about it as many observe at my blog http://88pianokeys.me/
- Strongly holds to the mantra "this is my studio, and I decide what happens", a favorite quote from Philip Johnston's book *The Dynamic Studio: How to Keep Students, Dazzle Parents, and Build the Studio Everyone Wants to Get Into*. I've decided that the iPad equips my studio with a dynamic learning environment and that it will be used on a regular basis
- Believes that since this is my book and I decide what happens, I will limit the content to iPad-friendly apps and will not be venturing out into the world of other tablets (unless someone twists my arm.)

WHO WOULD WANT TO READ THIS BOOK?

The book is intended for studio teachers (and other curious readers) who:

- Recognize the unique characteristics of the millennial generation and beyond
- See the need to set their studio apart and create a dynamic learning environment
- Have found the charm of the iPad too irresistible but need some guidance
- Wish to integrate technology into daily lessons and are looking for some sound advice.

BIOGRAPHY

Leila Viss holds a Master of Arts in Piano Performance and Pedagogy from the University of Denver. She enjoys teaching piano to around 45 students ranging in age from 6 to 90. She is drawn to discovering innovative teaching methods and successful practice strategies to encourage the average player to stick to the bench for life. Customizing lessons for each student is a priority and therefore she provides "blended" instruction of Classical, Jazz and Pop. The ever-changing tools of technology assist her in daily teaching. Every student not only has a private lesson but a lab session as well. Lab assignments include activities using the latest music software, MIDI, iPad apps, a Clavinova and more. She is co-author of the *Double Click Curriculum* for *The Celebrate Piano* method books published by Michelle Sisler from *Keys to Imagination*.

In 2012, she discovered a new "love" of blogging at 88pianokeys.me. The site includes a comprehensive music app directory and numerous app reviews. Her fascination with the iPad and apps resulted in this book, *The iPad Piano Studio: Keys to Unlocking the Power of Apps*. Invited by Pete Jutras, the editor of *Clavier Companion*, Leila now pens a column for the piano magazine called "Apps for Teaching."

Leila is a co-founder with Bradley Sowash - a jazz pianist, author and educator - of *88 Creative Keys*. This joint venture features camps, clinics and workshops for kids and adults to develop creativity. Their efforts to promote creative musicianship can be found at The Eye/Ear Revolution.com.

Leila has served on planning committees for the MTNA (Music Teachers National Association) 2013 Saturday Jazz/Pop Track, the MTNA 2014 Improvisation Track and was appointed co-chair of programs by Sam Holland for NCKP (National Conference on Keyboard Pedagogy) 2015.

Tom Folenta's magazine called *Simpletec* featured Leila in an article about her use of technology as a teacher. Although they had never met before, once introduced (thanks to their mutual friend and colleague, Shana Kirk) they discovered their diverse backgrounds and similar interests could create a dynamic team. With this discovery, their efforts have resulted in the publishing of this book and Tom and Leila will continue to provide high quality publications regarding technology in future print and digital editions at their site MTTCampus. com, Music Teachers Technology Campus.

When not teaching, writing, or planning, Leila is usually practicing the organ and piano for her church position, adjudicating piano and composition competitions and presenting at conferences.

Leila lives in Centennial, Colorado with her husband, Chuck, of 26 years, and three boys - two attend college and the youngest is in high school.

1 BEFORE WE GET STARTED

WHAT'S UP WITH THESE KIDS NOW A DAYS?

That's a good question. This latest generation is yet to have an official label; some call it Generation Z, Net-Geners, or Internet Generation. You probably know they like their gadgets, Youtube, video games and the Internet. Many experienced teachers and other sources reveal the nuances of working with today's students. Check out Barbara Kreader's articles in *Clavier Companion*. In a number of articles she has offered detailed descriptions of how she morphs her teaching to successfully connect with this "new breed" of students on the bench. She claims, "In the past, if a second-year student found himself unsure of note names or intervals, I whipped out flash cards, board games and notespellers. Today, I open my iPad to a music reading app..."[1] But before we look into this latest generation any further, perhaps it would be wise to take a look at your generation.

WE'RE SHARING THE GLOBE WITH 5 GENERATIONS?

A good friend of mine, Jeff VanKooten, is an outstanding speaker who has researched extensively the 5 generations alive today. His clever and insightful labels and descriptions can begin to help you understand yourself (just in case you were wondering):

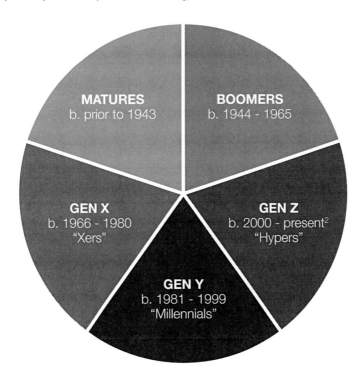

MATURES
b. prior to 1943

BOOMERS
b. 1944 - 1965

GEN X
b. 1966 - 1980
"Xers"

GEN Z
b. 2000 - present[2]
"Hypers"

GEN Y
b. 1981 - 1999
"Millennials"

[1] Barbara Kreader, "Teaching Music in a Virtual World," Clavier Companion Vol 5 No 1, (January/February 2013): 8. [2] Jeff Vankooten, *The Formative Themes that Shape Us*, http://jeffvankooten.com/?s=generations, (June 2012).

EACH GENERATION HAS A UNIQUE THEME?

Jeff claims there are four types of molding factors that shape us during our formative years (up to age 15). They include Adversity, Diversity, Economy and Technology.[3] Combine these factors into the mix of tags listed above and the resulting derivatives provide unique themes for the generations which all happen to begin with the letter C.[4]

1 The Matures experienced **CONFLICT** as in The Great Depression, World War II, etc.
2 Because of the number of Boomers (78 million), they found themselves in **CONTROL** and influencing society.
3 **CHAOS** describes the Xers as they were born during the Vietnam war, witnessed Watergate, and survived the energy crisis. "Certainty was an illusion."
4 **CHANGE** describes the experience of Millennials. Unimaginable innovations in technological growth and global shifts such as the Fall of the Berlin Wall and 9-11 have triggered a continual acceleration of change.
5 The youngest generation is flooded with **CHOICE**. Jeff suggests that because of the countless options available to these "Hypers", committing to just one "choice" may be difficult.[5]

HOW DO YOU LOCK INTO THE MINDS OF TODAY'S "HYPER" STUDENT?

There may be some implications for your personal approach as a studio teacher dependent upon your age group.

Matures might Re-evaluate the battles to be chosen and let go of (or at least not hold as tightly) the virtue of frugality and buy some technology. In other words, let go, and try the latest tech gadgets.

RE-EVALUATE

Boomers might Reconsider the need to supervise every detail at a lesson. Let the student's learning ebb and flow and explore with them the world of technology with a sense of wonder and not fear.

RECONSIDER

Xers might Resist the urge to hook into the latest fad and instead, stay steady to promote certain and steady progress.

RESIST

Millennials might Restrain themselves from all the latest gadgetry and focus in on what counts - making music.

RESTRAIN

BACK TO THE OPENING QUESTION, "WHAT'S UP WITH THESE KIDS NOW A DAYS?"

I'm guessing that most of you are Matures, Boomers, Xers and Millennials and are presently teaching Millennials and Hypers. (Come to think of it, I actually have a number of Boomers and even a couple of

---

[3] Jeff Vankooten, *The Formative Themes that Shape Us*, http://jeffvankooten.com/?s=generations, (June 2012). [4] Jeff Vankooten, *The Formative Themes that Shape Us*, http://jeffvankooten.com/?s=generations, (June 2012). [5] Jeff Vankooten, *The Formative Themes that Shape Us*, http://jeffvankooten.com/?s=generations, (June 2012).

Matures on the bench.) In any case, if Change and Choice characterize these younger generations, what does that mean for your studio and teaching style?

1 Every individual has a unique learning mode. We've known that for years. Using an iPad or computer program may be the perfect solution for one child while pencil and paper or hands-on at the keys may be best for another. Being prepared to offer a variety of alternatives for discovery at your studio will cater to the needs (and the desire to choose) of everyone.

2 Providing teacher-guided options in how concepts are introduced and which repertoire to perform will allow you to manage outcomes and will show you still care about students' preferences. Remember, with your skillfully selected options, you will still have control over your agenda, and the freedom to choose will keep students committed to the keys for the long-run. (That's the Boomer talking in me).

3 Outstanding technological tools are available that do more than just "dress up" or update your teaching methodology. These tools will truly enhance your instruction and student progress.

4 In his book, *The Dynamic Studio: How to Keep Students, Dazzle Parents and Build the Studio Everyone Wants*, Philip Johnston states that today's students have instant access to any activity, and spending time (too much time) on something (traditional structured piano lessons) that does not capture their attention may steal time for other easily accessed interests.

"The disjuncture between what our training has prepared us for and who we are actually working with has very real consequences for music teachers individually, and the profession as a whole." [6] - Johnston

Johnston claims that music teachers have two choices: "Accept higher attrition as a fact of life in today's modern teaching world, or rethink just what it is that their studio does so that it's not only able to attract today's students, but retain them."[7]

Will using an iPad and the latest technology help gain and retain students? I'd love to shout "YES!" to promote book sales but I can't make that promise. You and I both know it's the magical lure of making music that will keep students at the keys. Your willingness to engage in "their world" may be just the ticket to captivate budding musicians. Once you've got them on the bench, music can do "its job" and keep them there for a lifetime.

5 The home and love of parents and family and social environment also shape each generation. With all these labels and traits, we need to remember students are more than their gadgets; they are human beings with a desire to create. They signed up for lessons to learn how to make music on an instrument invented over 400 years ago. Technology is a tool, a resource, something that enhances learning and maybe even relationships. Remember, technology can never replace the exhilaration of making music - like drilling a tricky section until it's perfect, adding a crescendo that leads to the peak of a piece, creating an original work and the joy of a successful live performance.

That being said, let's move on to the iPad.

---

[6] Philip Johnston, *The Dynamic Studio: How to Keep Students, Dazzle Parents, and Build the Studio Everyone Wants* (Philip Johnston 2012), 9. [7] Philip Johnston, *The Dynamic Studio: How to Keep Students, Dazzle Parents, and Build the Studio Everyone Wants* (Philip Johnston 2012), 9.

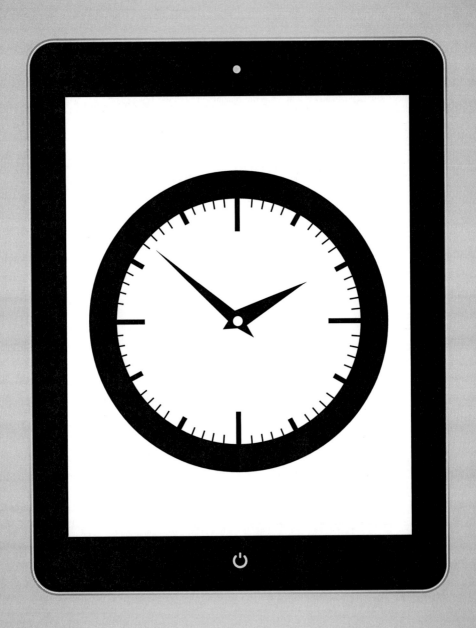

FINDING TIME TO USE THE iPAD IN A TYPICAL LESSON

THERE'S NEVER ENOUGH TIME IN A LESSON SO WHY NOT ADD LAB TIME ACTIVITIES IN ADDITION TO EACH PRIVATE LESSON?[1]

Fact: As mentioned in Chapter One, our studios are filled with those of the "Millennial", "Hyper" and "Generation Z" generations. They are known for their social networking, a cell phone in their pocket, body piercing, tattoos, global awareness and fascination in video games. With their daily immersion in modern technology, adding a lab will feed all the "comforts" (if you will) of these high-tech, high-maintenance generations.

Fact: Many schools have or will have iPads assigned to each student to use on a regular basis in addition to an ample supply of computers, online textbooks, etc. Some of my students have told me that an iPad will be a required "school supply" for next year (2013). I couldn't believe the number of students who arrived with iPhones and iPads after Christmas.

Fact: Technology continues to drive the direction of our society and learning styles. It is here to stay. Why NOT embrace it in your daily teaching?

SO NOW YOU MAY BE WONDERING: WHAT DO I MEAN BY A "LAB"?

When working towards my Masters Degree 20 years ago, I visited successful piano studios of many local prominent teachers. The studio that intrigued me the most was one that scheduled lessons at the piano along with tutorial lessons on the computer. When setting up my first in-home studio, I eagerly borrowed this lesson and lab format.

I do NOT have a large classroom with many keyboards and computers. I teach two students at a time, one is with me at the piano, one is working on a "lab" assignment at the computer or iPad in the same room. The pianist is facing away from the student completing lab work so there is little visual distraction.

WHAT ARE THE BENEFITS OF A LAB?

MORE INCOME: The suggested charge for a lab with a lesson is your present 30-min lesson rate plus 1/4 to 1/2 of that. If you currently charge $25 per lesson, adding a lab to each lesson could potentially raise your lesson rate to more than $35. This hourly rate can substantially increase your income, which in turn can support more advances in technology - specifically an iPad and plenty of apps.

MORE STUDENTS: Students who notice that you are willing to meet them where they are with an adventuresome spirit into the world of technology will be attracted to your studio. This will (yes it will) increase the number of applicants on your wait list.

MORE TIME: Of all the benefits, time is the biggest bonus in my opinion. There is more time for:

- **Student Creativity:** Often this gets placed on the back burner so that the essentials can be addressed during a lesson. With lab time, there is so much more opportunity for creative assignments.

[1] Leila Viss, *Adding a Lab to your Lesson*, http://www.composecreate.com/adding-a-lab-to-your-lessons-why/, (April 2012). Portions of this chapter are taken from a series of 5 articles written by me specifically for ComposeCreate.com.

- **Teacher Creativity:** The fact that weekly lab activities must be planned for every student continues to provide variety in instruction. There is never a dull moment ever again for you or your pianists.

- **Dimension:** Learning styles vary and so will your versatility of instruction with the addition of lab assignments away from the bench.

- **Relationships:** Sharing a lesson time with another student fosters piano peers which is unique, as playing the piano can often be a "lonely" activity.

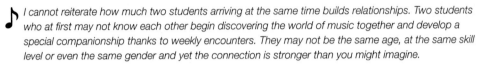

I cannot reiterate how much two students arriving at the same time builds relationships. Two students who at first may not know each other begin discovering the world of music together and develop a special companionship thanks to weekly encounters. They may not be the same age, at the same skill level or even the same gender and yet the connection is stronger than you might imagine.

MORE PROGRESS: With more time, teacher and students can build a relationship of trust within an environment of fun, which enhances learning and progress. I have no scientific proof of this but believe it is true from my personal experience.

HOW DO I MARKET THIS LAB IDEA?

You will need a list of convincing arguments to use when marketing this new lesson format to parents and potential new families. Here are some to consider:

- The student will receive twice as much time with you than before but the parent will be paying less than twice the price. When parents begin shopping for teachers and see that by paying a little more, their child will receive a longer time of instruction, I often "win over" the family. In a few cases, students have enrolled elsewhere because the parents were concerned about sharing a lesson time with another child. I understand that it could be seen as a disadvantage, but honestly, sharing the lesson hour offers few negative situations in my opinion.

- If the budding musician seems apprehensive about learning the piano, seeing that other tools and "toys" are involved may lure him/her to the keys.

- For those who enroll siblings, the convenience factor is huge. Parents receive a two-for-one drop off! In many cases, even THREE for one. Currently I have families that enroll 3 siblings. I've agreed to see all three at the same time and have devised three rotations to keep them busy. The parents eagerly complete the drop-off and have admitted the kids are barely slamming the car door shut before they zip off eager to take advantage of free time away from three!

- The benefits listed above provide even more marketing material – More time for Creativity, Dimension and Relationships, which I know result in more progress.

HOW WILL CURRENT STUDENTS FAMILIES REACT TO THIS NEW ADDITION?

- Perhaps the most difficult part of initiating a new lesson format and tuition rate would be informing those who are currently enrolled in your studio. It will be an adjustment and you may lose some students. However, usually today's parents recognize that technology is an essential part of school curriculums and most will be enthusiastic that you echo the use of those same tools in your studio.

- Lab sessions are required for all my K-12 students although lesson formats vary with age and skill level. Enforce the same policy for all in your studio and get everyone on board.

- Communication of this new format will be crucial and nothing demonstrates your tech-savvy, 21st-century studio better than a fine website.

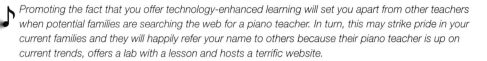 *Promoting the fact that you offer technology-enhanced learning will set you apart from other teachers when potential families are searching the web for a piano teacher. In turn, this may strike pride in your current families and they will happily refer your name to others because their piano teacher is up on current trends, offers a lab with a lesson and hosts a terrific website.*

WHAT ARE THE DRAWBACKS TO THIS NEW FORMAT?

- You will need to develop strong skills in multi-tasking with two (or three) students requiring your attention. Usually, I walk through the lab assignment with them first. As I get one up and running with the correct app or website and headphones, I ask the other to play through one of his/her assigned pieces.

- Technology can be flakey. You need to be ready to trouble shoot and have plan B in place, especially if you rely on the computer for online games or software. The iPad serves as a marvelous Plan B as apps are always available. Software may not load, the Internet may be spotty, so the iPad (thankfully) offers wonderful opportunities for such occurrences. I cannot express how the addition of the iPad has reinvigorated my lab assignments. (You'll be reading more about why, soon).

- Families will need to adjust to a new tuition rate and some may not be happy, at least for a little while. However, plan to attract more students with a tech-savvy studio.

WHERE DO I BEGIN?

If this "lab-plus-a-lesson" idea has grabbed your attention, I highly recommend the book *Studio Makeover: Technology Addition*[2] by Michelle Sisler. This manual will be your best friend and hold your hand during the many steps I have briefly mentioned above. *Note: It even includes a sample letter to send your parents announcing your exciting new venture. You are not alone. There are plenty of resources on and off line to make this a reality in your studio. I am willing to help however I can.*

HOW DO I FIT THIS IN? SCHEDULING LESSONS IS HARD ENOUGH ALREADY!

Essentially, two students will be scheduled per hour. Instead of one arriving at 3:30 and then another at 4:00pm, both students would arrive at 3:30 and leave at 4:30. Some of my high school students schedule a 45 min lesson (due to their level of repertoire) with a 15-minute lab time. I do not have as many of these students and they usually arrive early (2:30pm) before most K-8 students. After setting up the high school student with a lab assignment, I use those precious 15 minutes to check emails, get a snack (and go to the bathroom!) before the line-up of 30/30min students arrives at 3:30pm.

[2] Michelle Sisler, *Studio Makeover: Technology Addition* (Keys to Imagination, 2008), 15.

WHAT TOOLS ARE ESSENTIAL TO GET THIS UP AND RUNNING?

Most likely you will already own the basic equipment:

- **COMPUTER/LAPTOP:** I am an Apple fan (can you tell?) but PCs work as well with most software and of course any online sites.

- **HEADPHONES:** I have had little trouble with the set I purchased from Guitar Center, but headphones can break (you know how kids can be) so invest in a good pair. I do know that some teachers have asked students to provide their own headphones to avoid major replacement expenses.
  Note: It can get a little noisy as I am teaching in the same room while the student is completing a lab assignment; however, there are really few complaints thanks to headphones that cover the ear entirely.

- **INTERNET CONNECTION:** Even though it's not necessary to run every app with an Internet connection, there are some good apps that do require a connection and it seems this may continue to build in popularity.

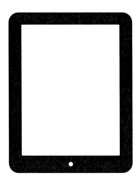

- **iPAD:** In the past, I would have said a lab is only possible with a computer. Now, I believe that if you have an iPad with the right apps, your lab could be complete, even if you have NO computer available.

- **SUPPORT:** Do not be bashful, ask for help early and often. The Apple Store offers One to-One workshops and the Genius Bar. Microsoft has stores and support as well. My husband is a computer "guru" (PC not Mac) so his assistance is always appreciated. I attend conferences and I eagerly make friends with those who are clearly more "tech savvy" than me. Find other teachers in your area who have a lab, use an iPad or wish to begin a lab. Work together by exchanging information and ideas.

My intention is that this book will not only promote the use of an iPad also but inspire each reader to consider enhancing every lesson with the addition of technology. It continues to set my studio apart; it could do the same for yours.

> *"The Static Studio laments that they can't afford to keep up with technology. The Dynamic Studio knows that they can't afford not to."*[3]
>
> - Philip Johnston

WHAT IF I JUST CAN'T COMMIT TO THIS LAB IDEA? CAN THE iPAD BE A USEFUL ADDITION TO PRIVATE AND GROUP LESSONS?

By all means, yes. There are more and more apps I use during the lesson such as iReal b, Octavian Basics, Anytune and more. Stay tuned; upcoming chapters will focus on incredibly useful ways to enhance daily lesson time, not just lab time.

[3] Philip Johnston, *The Dynamic Studio: How to Keep Students, Dazzle Parents and Build the Music Studio Everyone Wants to Get Into* (Philip Johnston, 2012), 256.

3 STILL CONTEMPLATING

WHY SHOULD I PURCHASE AN iPAD FOR MY STUDIO?

If you are reading this book perhaps you:

- May have already purchased an iPad but are wondering what you got yourself into
- Are reluctant and skeptical, wondering what all the hype is about and still debating the benefit of purchasing an iPad
- Are intrigued with the slick technology of the iPad but fearful of the steep learning curve and the price tag
- Are ready to jump on the iPad bandwagon but need some support with your newly acquired technology.

To be blunt, the purpose of this book is to encourage you not only to purchase an iPad but also to be an iConvert, one who is just as fascinated with the iPad and its capabilities for you and your studio as I am. After reading the following chapters, you may recognize that the iPad is not the tool for you (hope not). Either way, you will find answers to help you decide which path to follow.

THERE ARE MANY TABLETS OUT THERE. WHY THE iPAD?

I visited many sites that compared Android tablets to the iPad. Repeatedly, a choice to purchase an iPad over a competitor came down to two reasons:

1 It's an Apple Product.
2 The App Store.

Apple knows how to make a fabulous tablet (using the same operating system of the popular iPhone) and Apple has some of the best apps – more than any other tablet app store. (Washington Post)[1] "Programmers had been developing apps for the iPad for nearly a year before the other tablets appeared. The Apple App Store was bursting with thousands of programs while the Android app store was nearly empty". (How Stuff Works)[2]

And one more fan gives his reasons why Apple is the way to go. From Paul Shimmons:

> *"First and foremost...they work. Second....they are fast and reliable. Third...Apple has won the number one slot in Fortune's annual "World's Most Admired Companies" list for the sixth year in a row. That's not by accident."*[3]

[1] Hayley Tsukayama, *The New iPad: 5 Reasons to By, 5 Reasons Not To*, http://www.washingtonpost.com/business/technology/the-new-ipad-5-reasons-to-buy-5-reasons-not-to/2012/03/09/glQAmB9b1R_story.html ,(March 2012). [2] Christopher Lampton, *iPad vs Android Tablets*, http://computer.howstuffworks.com/tablets/ipad-vs-android-tablets.html, (December 2011). [3] Paul Shimmons, Why Would I Suggest Apple Products?, http://ipadmusiced.wordpress.com/2013/02/28/why-would-i-suggest-apple-products/, (February 2013).

IS IT WORTH THE INVESTMENT?

When introducing the iPad 2, Steve Jobs stated,

"Technology alone is not enough. It is technology married with liberal arts, married with the humanities that yields us the result that makes our hearts sing."[4]

I don't "sing" about my iPad regularly, however…Jobs' description of the iPad's aesthetic look and functionality is really not an exaggeration. The chart below lists some of items that the iPad can replace which in turn will save you hundreds and hundreds of dollars in time and efficiency.

AUDIO LIBRARY	INTERNET SURFER
BENEFIT All your existing iTunes content (audio books, tunes from your CD library, movies) travel with you in one slim device.	Searching for composer info or the perfect YouTube video is only a finger tip away.
VALUE Save shelf space, time and energy when locating a recording.	Gain instant access to info to create a dynamic lesson experience.

[4] Jonah Lehrer, Steve Jobs: *"Technology Alone is Not Enough"*, http://www.newyorker.com/online/blogs/newsdesk/2011/10/steve-jobs-pixar.html, (October 2011).

PRINT LIBRARY	**CAMERA**
BENEFIT All digital books, magazines, pdfs and digital scores are accessed on ONE large, high resolution display. The need for a book bag is eliminated.	Both still shots and video can be captured and shared easily.
VALUE Spare space and store volumes of books in a virtual book shelf.	Cross off the expense of a video camera.

Meet your personal and studio needs with an all-in-one unit! The diversity of the iPad is limited only by your imagination thanks to the ongoing efforts of app developers. With all of that capability, an iPad (and accompanying apps) can hardly be considered a poor investment. Furthermore, the immersion of technology and education that an iPad provides has resulted in a paradigm shift in how schools and teachers and - I dare say piano teachers? - educate.

HOW MUCH STORAGE WILL I NEED?

The iPad comes in mixed storage capacities: 16 GB, 32 GB, 64 GB or greater. I have only purchased the 16GB because I was hesitant to spend money on extra storage. As I collect more and more apps, I KNOW I will spring for the space on my next one since I like to take and edit videos with my iPad. According to an article by Josh Smith, it's important for you to know or at least predict how you will use the iPad first before you purchase. That will ultimately guide you in determining the storage space you need. I'm guessing that you will become an "app addict" like me and wish to purchase many, as they are inexpensive and so handy. If that's the case, listen to Smith's suggestion:

"App sizes are going to climb once developers start pushing out new iPad versions to take advantage of the Retina Display. If you love apps, especially beautiful apps, I suggest starting at the 32GB iPad and going up to 64GB if you can afford it, especially if you plan to keep music or movies on your iPad as well."[5]

Before you do, learn more about iCloud in Chapter Four.

SHOULD I PLAN TO REPLACE MY COMPUTER WITH AN iPAD?

The iPad is a nifty, efficient device that can stand alone. However, I still use heavy-duty programs and significant memory space that only a computer can support (at this time). Remember, the iPad has limitations as it has no internal hard drive. Keep your computer but supplement your technology needs and boost your tech "savviness" with an iPad.

ONCE I BUY AN iPAD, DO I NEED ANYTHING ELSE?

Yes...

- An Apple ID and account if you wish to purchase books, music and apps.
- Internet access.
- A computer, even though it really is not needed anymore thanks to the ability to update an iPad wirelessly (without a computer) you'll find many tasks easier with one.
- You'll want to purchase some apps.
- Oh, and there are some accessories that you will not want to pass up.

CAN'T I DO ALL THE SAME THINGS WITH MY iPHONE?

Yes, the iPhone can do most anything the iPad can but honestly, size does matter. The 7 x 9.5 screen of the iPad allows for easy viewing. If your eyesight is not always reliable like mine, this can come in very handy. For small children, bigger is better. Besides, do you really want students using your iPhone? In addition, there are apps specifically made for the iPad. The iPad features a Retina display that creates sharper images and a mobile "chip" that delivers quick response. iPad apps are designed to take

[5] Josh Smith, *Which App Should I Buy?*, http://www.gottabemobile.com/2012/03/12/which-ipad-should-i-buy-16gb-vs-32gb-vs-64gb/, (March 2012).

advantage of these technologies built into the device. Plus, with 10 hours of battery life, you don't need to worry about the device dying during the middle of your busy teaching afternoon.

BEFORE I DIVE INTO THE NEXT CHAPTERS, CAN YOU GIVE ME A COUPLE OF HINTS ON HOW OWNING AN iPAD WILL REVOLUTIONIZE MY STUDIO?

Sure. Perhaps the best analogy is to think of the iPad as an award-winning movie star. This actor has undergone advanced training and has the ability to shift roles in a couple of taps and a swipe or two.

The roles are extensive, making the iPad worthy of a STAR on Hollywood Boulevard. Here's a short list...

Back-Up Band

Business Manager

Doodle Pad

Metronome

Movie Screen

Paper Saver

Recording Studio

Three Ring Binder for Sheet Music

Video Arcade

Video Teacher

...and so much more.

Get comfy and settle in for a good show.

"A tool is a transparent cable connecting Purpose to Results. If you even see the tool, you missed the point." - Carl King[6]

[6] Carl King: *So, You're A Creative Genius (Now What...)* (Micahel Wiese Productions, 2011), p54.

PLEASE EXPLAIN: A HANDY GLOSSARY & HELPFUL TIPS

WHAT IF I DON'T SPEAK THIS LANGUAGE?

Perhaps entering the technology world would not be so daunting if there weren't so many new vocabulary words to memorize. Those who are tech-savvy and immersed in the world of technology assume you, me, anyone, are also well-versed in all tech terminology. I find this assumption to be prohibitive. It creates a steep intimidation factor which can easily frighten away even the most curious. Remember, this book is based on my experience and not my expertise so believe me when I say I have looked to other sources to answer these questions for myself as well as for your benefit. As the information is general common knowledge maybe to most, I won't include too many footnotes, and of course more information is easily accessed online at Apple.com.

WHAT DOES iOS STAND FOR?

iOS is a mobile operating system developed and distributed exclusively by Apple,Inc. It was originally released for the iPhone and now supports other Apple products as well. Apple does not allow their iOS to be installed on any other hardware. New updated operating systems are released periodically, thus the numbers iOS 5 and iOS 6 and now the iOS 7. This book was written while using the iOS 6. From all accounts, the latest Apple operating system includes massive changes in features and looks which means you may wish to hold off on installing the iOS 7 until those nasty bugs are fixed. As promised, I plan to offer ongoing support beyond this book so we can step through this new iOS 7 steep learning curve together.

WHAT IS AN APP?

- A slang term for an iPhone or iPad "application"
- "App" doesn't fall far from the "Apple" tree (pun intended)
- Could be thought of as software sold as a units or small portions.

WHAT DOES "STORAGE" MEAN?

In your studio, you need to store books, instruments, pencils, etc. Likewise, the iPad needs a place to store apps, any documents, photos and videos, etc. The size of "closet space" you prefer may be directly related to how much you want to spend on that "extra room" as storage gets pricey, especially on the higher end 64G models. Although it seems strange to spend extra money on "free or open" space it may be something to consider when you purchase an iPad if you plan to store a great deal of music, videos and apps. Just so you know, my next iPad will be one with more storage rather than less.

iOS7   iOS6

WHAT IS iCLOUD?

If you prefer to limit what you spend on storage for your iPad, there is space provided in the "attic" so to speak. This "invisible" storage system is Apple's "sync" service, which allows you to view all apps, photos and documents on your computer and any iDevice. Here's an explanation from the *MacWorld* staff that says it better than I can:

"When Steve Jobs spoke about iCloud, he said that Apple was going to demote the computer to be "just another device." So, rather than your Mac [computer] being the digital hub for your media and personal information, that job would be taken over by online services - specifically, iCloud. Given that now many of us have not only multiple computers but also one or more mobile computing devices such as the iPhone, iPod touch, and iPad, this makes a lot of sense. Coordinating all your information between these devices has become a chore - particularly when you attempt to do it all from a single computer. The promise of iCloud is that syncing media and data will "just work." Just enter your Apple ID on your various devices and iCloud will make sure that all those devices have the most up-to-date content on them."[1]

Your iPad comes with 5GB of storage and of course you always can purchase more in the iCloud, all with your Apple ID and account.

WHAT IS iTUNES?

Think of it as two things: First, it is a built-in app - already downloaded to your iPad - that functions as a library to store music and more. Second, it is an online store in which you can purchase music, movies, audio books, etc. Apple developed this media library application to play, store, download and organize music and videos. You'll need to download this app if you do not have it on your computer. When you tap on your "Music" icon on your iPad you will see your personal library of songs and playlists. When you tap on the iTunes icon, you can travel to the online store where you are able to purchase new music, audio books, movies, etc. Again, you will need an Apple ID and account.

WHERE'S THE APP STORE?

No need to hop in the car as access to the store is only a fingertip away. A single tap on the built-in icon labeled "App Store" will allow you to begin shopping for an app in seconds. Don't forget your Apple ID!

WHAT IS "SYNCING"?

When you plug your iPad into your computer, the two devices will synchronize or be able to transfer music, apps, photos, etc. This syncing can now be done wirelessly as well (no need to connect to the computer as this will be completed when your iPad is charging!).

---

[1] http://www.macworld.com/article/1160380/icloud_what_you_need_to_know.html, iCloud: What you Need to Know June 8, 2011.

WHAT'S AN APPLE ID?

An Apple ID is an important element with the purchase of any iDevice. You must '
more importantly, you must remember your Apple ID password. To shop at the i
Store you are required to set up an account with an email address and a passwo...
your iDevice, the Apple Store (if that's where the iPad is purchased) is more than happy to help ,
up this account. I've noticed a trend: as more and more students secure the latest iDevices, they bring
their iPads to lessons eager to download recommended apps. However, some find themselves locked
out of the App store. In their haste to set up their account, they forget their password or forget where
they wrote it down.

*Ahem...the above scenario does have something to do with the age of these students. These particularly
forgetful students are well beyond 40-something but have willingly dived into the iDevice world. The
learning curve is steep and passwords are forgotten because there are just too many for them to
remember. I wish I could help step them through this process when they first purchase an iDevice and
remind them about the importance of KNOWING their Apple ID. Thankfully, there is help online or at
the Apple store if a password is forgotten, but, it does slow down the app-purchase process. I am very
thankful for my loyal, adult students who continue to enhance their life with piano lessons; however, a
few of the lessons have been more about the iPad as of late. Regardless, they always go home with
something new to practice.*

IS THERE A WAY TO KEEP ALL THESE APPS ORGANIZED?

To find an app on the iPad you might find yourself swiping from screen to screen. Here are the steps to
develop a filing system which will help you "tidy-up" your iPad.

- Tap and hold on the icon of an app until it wiggles.
- Drag that app with your fingertip over the top of another similar app. A file folder will be created and
  Apple will suggest a name for the folder.
- To change the file title to a name you prefer, tap the X on the bar where the folder name appears and
  type in a new name.
- Continue to tap and drag similar apps to that folder.
- If you have an app on the second page but want to move it into a file folder on the first page of your
  iPad, tap and hold on the icon until it wiggles, then move it down to your main menu (where your mail,
  safari, photos icons live). Then swipe to the page where the desired folder appears and drag the
  wiggling icon to its new home.
- To **STOP** the icons from wiggling, press your **HOME** button.

Happy house cleaning!

HOW DO I LOCATE ALL THE ESSENTIAL SWITCHES AND SOCKETS?

This streamlined device is so sleekly designed that it can be a little difficult to find the right button or port when you need it. My students have laughed at me as I've tried to plug in headphones in the wrong place. Since the screen flips as you turn it from side to side, it is difficult to determine which end is "up". So, I'm bound and determined to get acquainted with important buttons and ports and memorize their location relative to the home button.

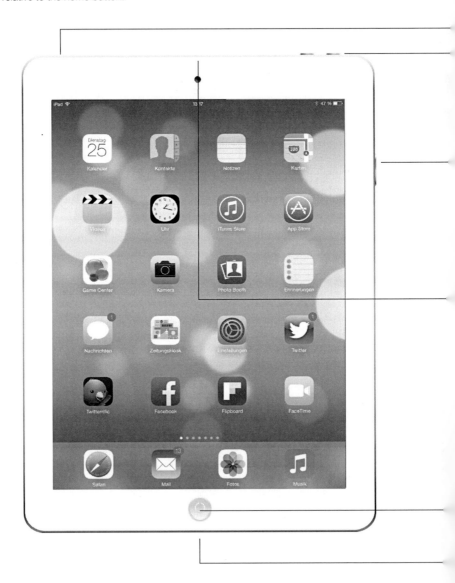

- **HEADPHONE JACK:** When students use the iPad during lab time, I provide headphones, not ear buds. They snap in just like the buds in to the designated port.

- **SLEEP/WAKE:** Your iPad likes to doze to save power and with one tap on this button it sleeps immediately. Press and hold this button to turn it completely off. It's good to know where this button is particularly when the flight attendant is walking by to ensure that "all electronic hand-held devices are turned off" prior to landing.

- **VOLUME:** Like a teeter-totter--holding down one side will turn up the volume, the other side will turn it down. In my mind, it's always a guessing game which way is which. Be flexible.

- **MICROPHONE:** This feature is essential to recording so make sure to know where this is located before you hit the "record" button.

- **HOME BUTTON:** Really, this is the only button on the whole machine that you can noticeably see. Click this to turn on or wake up your iPad or to close an app and return to the home screen.

- **DOCK CONNECTOR:** Probably the 2nd most important element to know about your iPad after the home button, this port is where you insert the cable to connect your iPad to an outlet for recharging, the computer for syncing, and many additional devices. Learn more about special connection adaptors and accessories in Chapter 11.

VIDEO QR ▶

5   THE iPAD IS PURCHASED AND OUT OF THE BOX

I'M SOLD ON THE iPAD AND MAYBE EVEN A LAB, SO NOW WHAT?

Although there are countless (I mean way too many) software programs and off-the-bench activities I could include here for lab and lesson assignments, this book will be limited to activities and utilities specifically designed around the use of the iPad.

The main purpose of lesson and lab time is to educate your budding musician. If you choose to invest in technology, you'll want to make sure it's beneficial for both you and the student. I must say from personal experience that it is easy to "fall in love" with the iPad and accompanying apps, which may distract you from the real purpose of your investment: to complement your business and teaching. In addition, due to the enormous amount of apps, one can become overwhelmed. Be patient, remain calm and STAY FOCUSED!

> *"Don't get seduced by the gadgets themselves. Look instead at the teaching solutions they make possible, and then rank those--in the end it's solutions you're purchasing and not gadgetry."*[1] *-Philip Johnston*

ARE THERE FREE APPS INCLUDED WITH A PURCHASE OF AN iPAD?

Yes, so before you roll your cart into the App Store and begin emptying the shelves, let's take a look at the apps already built-in to your device. I would hardly call them "free"; however, they are there for your benefit immediately upon purchase so get to know them.

Apple.com provides a very nice listing and thorough explanation of all your built-in apps. Please refer to the site for details. The apps I list below are included here because I include a personal tip or two.

iOS7   iOS6

    SAFARI

This is your Internet browser. Among other tools of this browser, my favorite is the Reading List. After you've Googled "Apple.com" or "88pianokeys" on Safari, you may find that you do not have time to read about the features of the iPad or my latest blog about a favorite app. Tap on the book icon and you will see a list of **Bookmarks**. Click on **Reading List** and then the "+" sign and the page or blog will be added to your list. You can visit your reading list in the future and easily find that blog you wanted to read.

---

[1] Philip Johnston, *The Dynamic Studio: How to Keep Students, Dazzle Parents, and Build the Studio Everyone Wants* (PracticeSpot Press, 2012), 254.

MAIL

Here you will be able to create, read, and reply to emails from your mail accounts. Apple's email system supports Google, Yahoo, Hotmail and others. When I have to check emails fast from any of my three accounts, I find the iPad incredibly handy and emails are large enough to read easily.

  iBOOKS

Tapping this icon will allow you to:

1 Visit the book store and purchase books available at the iBookstore by tapping on "Store".

2 View books in your library by tapping on "Collections". Besides books, I also store and organize Pdf docs from the web such as manuals, handouts, and music scores.

  PHOTOS

As you might guess, this is where all your photos are stored in a place so they can be viewed, organized, even edited and presented as a slideshow. One unique feature of the iPad is that it seems to work "backwards" (at least in my opinion) from how you may be accustomed to operating. For example, when you wish to create an album of a number of photos, first click on the word *Album*, then *Edit*, then *New Album*. You will be prompted to tap on any photo to add to the album.

  FACETIME

A "Skype-like" app that makes video calls with others that own iDevices. This could be terrific for make-up lessons for those who call in sick if the family has a Facetime-friendly device AND IF your studio policies allow for such lessons.

  MAPS

When you need to find your way, this app can help. As of 2013, most agree that the Google Maps app still reigns supreme.

  MUSIC

Tapping on this icon at the bottom of your screen directs you to your music library - not to be confused with the iTunes icon that takes you to the iTunes store.

NEWSSTAND

These shelves hold all your newspaper and article subscriptions. This is where the *Clavier Companion* digital edition and other favorite magazines are stored.

SIRI

I currently do not own an iPad with Siri, however my husband has "her" on his iPhone 5. Although it could be handy, after my husband tried it a couple of times, he hasn't used it since. I've heard others say they use Siri to text hands-free when driving, call up directions to a location and more. Some teachers use Siri with young students who do not read. The young pianists simply make a verbal request to Siri for a particular app and it loads. Wow, great idea!

A "SUITE OF OFFICE UTILITIES" INCLUDING iMESSAGE, CALENDAR, REMINDERS AND CONTACTS

Provides a great place to communicate, store student information, make to-do lists and manage your schedule. Because I use www.MusicTeachersHelper.com, I rarely use these apps. However, I find them easy to use and could be potentially helpful for your business. More on that later.

NOTES

A favorite of mine because of its simplicity. Here's where I keep lists for book orders or any other notes to self that I need to jot down in a hurry. They even show up in my Apple account mailbox.

APP STORE

One-stop shopping for all your app needs - no driving OR postage necessary as clicking on the icon takes you immediately to the App store. Just type in the app your want in the search window and it will be "brought" to you. Make sure to know and "carry" your Apple ID!

iTUNES

Shop for music and movies here and also find your iTunes on your computer to keep your iPad in sync with software updates, tunes and more. However, this has become almost unnecessary thanks to the wireless updating standard with all iPad 2's and beyond.

CAMERA

The High Definition camera of my iPad 3 is SO addictive. Recording a video is easy and sending it to parents via email or uploading to YouTube is a breeze. The remarkable combination of an HD camera (standard on the iPad 3) and your OWN YouTube channel is a MUST for your studio.

DID YOU SAY "MY OWN YOUTUBE CHANNEL?"

Yes, I said YouTube channel. You can create your own. First you need a YouTube Account. Go to YouTube.com and they will step you through the information needed (essentially your email and a password but things get even easier if you already have a Google account as Google owns YouTube).

♪ *Since purchasing my iPad 1 and 3, the YouTube app is no longer a default app on the home screen. If the YouTube app is not on your screen, plan to stop at the App store and pick this one up!*

Once you have an account, your YouTube home page offers a menu of options including:

1 Subscriptions: YouTube is THE place to find out what others are performing, teaching, and creating. If you find a video you like while browsing, you can subscribe to the "Channel" that it comes from, and YouTube will give you a weekly update of the latest videos from all your subscriptions.

2 Playlists: To keep your videos organized, create playlist titles and move videos to the appropriate list.

If you shoot videos of your own, the iPad makes it easy to move them to Youtube.

1 Find and tap on your Camera icon on your iPad to take a video (make sure to click on the video camera icon on the bottom right side). After completing your video shoot, you may wish to use the option to trim your video at the top of the screen. Touch the long box of images of your video and wait for it to turn yellow. Slide the bar until you are happy with the edited video content. Next, click on the "forward arrow" and you will have three choices: mail the video, message it or send it to YouTube.

2 At the top right of the screen, there is a box "Upload" where you can add your own videos to your channel.

3 Click on **YouTube** and it will prompt you to enter a title, description, tags, and category. You also can decide if you wish the video to be public, unlisted or private. I would suggest selecting Public or Unlisted for ease of viewing if you wish to share videos with others. After entering the desired information for the video, simply push Publish and after a couple of minutes, depending on the size of the video, your video will be uploaded to your YouTube channel. Really, it is THAT simple.

Though privacy issues are a concern, I always make videos public anyway so they are easier to share. If I post a video of a student, I only include his/her first name. To secure parental permission, I ask student families to sign a permission statement included in the fall registration. Once videos are posted, I organize them into playlists. In my experience, most of the people who view the videos were directed to YouTube from my site so they aren't really strangers. Although there may be some nosey peeps lurking out there, I believe most will find other channels more interesting than mine.

Marking a video as "private" effectively claims that it's not "interesting" to the general public and if that were the case, why would I encourage you to create a YouTube channel? Because this is one of the best technological tools you can use to inspire your students. If they have a piece that is performance ready, pull out the iPad, record it, send it to Youtube and email to mom and dad even before the student returns home. You know how much value there is in observing one's own performance? Further more, proud parents eagerly share the link of their young pianist performing with friends and relatives. Nothing can set your studio apart more quickly then an instant recording studio offered so conveniently by YOU (and your iPad).

If you desire more in-depth information about using Youtube to enhance your teaching, this book catapulted me into the world of Youtube: *Youtube in Music Education* by Thomas Rudolph and James Frankel.

Here's a Sample Release Form from Natalie Wickham's *Music Matter's* Blog:

"I, _____, hereby grant permission for my child, _____, born on _____, to have his/her photo and/or video used by Natalie's Piano Studio in promotional materials, downloadable products, website content, and blog posts."

Parent Signature _____ Date _____[2]

It is important to remember that this is YOUR studio and YOUR iPad so never force yourself beyond your comfort zone. Be prepared for a steep learning curve, stay steady, and plan to plateau. Integrate more tech-savvy instruction when YOU are ready. Although I may own a large number of apps, their price tag allows me to sit on them for a while and then pick up one (when I need it) to enhance my teaching. Watch your beginners learn to play the piano. Notice how much repetition is required to build skills. Set your sights on reasonable goals, perhaps taking baby steps, when immersing yourself in new technology. Rome was not built in a day and Beethoven's "Moonlight Sonata" is nowhere to be found in method book one.

"The <u>Static</u> Studio uses technology to keep up with what other studios offer. The <u>Dynamic</u> Studio mines technology for teaching options that no other teaching studio has even thought of yet."[3] -Philip Johnston

[2] Natalie Wickham, *Media Release Form*, http://musicmattersblog.com/2012/12/10/monday-mailbag-media-release-forms-for-piano-students/ , (December 2012). [3] Philip Johnston, *The Dynamic Studio: How to Keep Students, Dazzle Parents, and Build the Studio Everyone Wants* (PracticeSpot Press, 2012), 273.

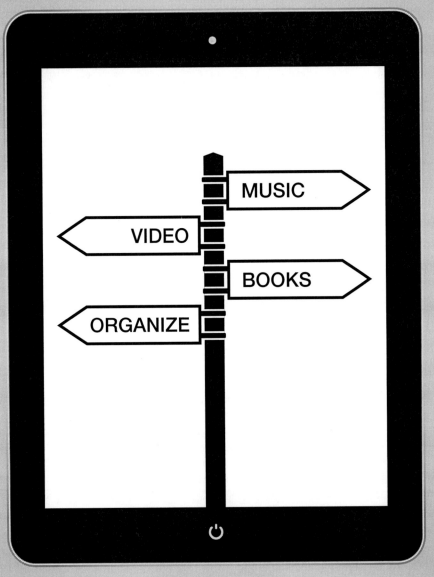

VIDEO QR ▶

6 FINDING THE RIGHT APPS

I'M READY TO GO TO THE APP STORE SO HOW DO I DECIDE WHAT TO PURCHASE FIRST?

This question alone is perhaps the sole reason for this book. Once the initial love affair of the iPad wore off, I felt it was time to make sense of it all. FYI: there are WAY too many apps available. Honestly, if you are looking for an app for a particular purpose it can feel like searching for a needle in a haystack. Therefore, it's good to have the advice of others that have scouted out the hunt in the haystack before you.

IS THERE A GUIDE FOR FINDING APPROPRIATE APPS FOR THE MUSIC STUDIO?

For a detailed list, check out 88pianokeys.me. Early on in my blogging career, I decided to do myself (and my readers) a favor by creating a Music iPad App Directory. Anyone who knows me at all knows that I love to organize. Once it became apparent that acquiring apps useful to the music studio could be addicting but also overwhelming, I took it upon myself to sort through, evaluate and assign apps to a "category" after each one was purchased.

As I've embarked on this endeavor, I've come to realize that my mission will be impossible to complete. Since there will never be enough time for me to make in-depth investigations of EVERY app, and as apps continue to develop and change, I compile blog posts written by *other* respected bloggers and include links in my Music App Directory. So take advantage of my acquaintance with apps and the Music App Directory at 88pianokeys.me. In addition, because you have purchased this book you will also have access to continued support, ie: the videos included in this book with more to come.

ONCE I PURCHASE A RECOMMENDED APP, IS THERE A PLACE TO KEEP IT SO I CAN FIND IT EASILY ON MY IPAD?

Thankfully the iPad provides a way to organize your apps according to the "category" you assign them. Below are the category labels I've come up with so far. I say "so far" because by the time this book is published, I may have changed names of categories or added new ones. Determining these names definitely depends upon personal preference. Think of categories as folders that store similar apps in one place. It is hoped that my Music App Directory and category names will enhance your experience as you become good, no, best friends with your iPad.

MY APP CATEGORIES

Books	Creativity	Ear Training
Early Theory	Flash Cards	Just Plain Fun
Note Reading	Organize	Productivity

- Camera
- Scores
- Power Tools
- History
- Sight Reading
- Theory
- Metronome
- Social
- with MORE to come
- Rhythm
- Store

ONCE I ASSIGN AN APP TO A CATEGORY, HOW DO I KEEP ALL SIMILAR APPS IN THE SAME FOLDER?

(As a refresher, I've included this info here even though these steps were featured in an earlier chapter.)

Here are the steps to "tidy-up" your apps into the appropriate folder:

- Tap and hold on the icon of an app until it wiggles.
- Drag that app with your fingertip over the top of another similar app. A file folder will be created and Apple will suggest a name for the folder.
- To change the file title to a name you prefer, tap the X on the bar where the folder name appears and type in a new name.
- Continue to tap and drag similar apps to that folder.
- If you have an app on the second page but want to move it into a file folder on the first page of your iPad, tap and hold on the icon until it wiggles, then move it down to your main menu (where your Mail, Safari, Photos icons live). Then swipe to the page where the desired folder appears and drag the wiggling icon to its new home.
- To STOP the icons from wiggling, press your HOME button.
- Tip: My folders are in alphabetical order on my first page for easy reference.

Happy house cleaning!

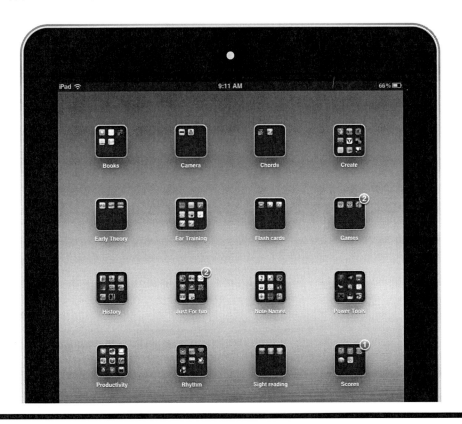

7 YOU'VE JUST HIRED A NEW ASSISTANT

DISCLAIMER: *Due to the constant changes in the world of technology, what you are about to read is not anywhere close to being complete or up to date. If I really like an app, I write about how I use it in my column, "One App at a Time" at 88PianoKeys.me. It is my intent that this collection of "stories" about my app experiences will spur you to explore individual apps yourself. This will help you secure the apps that work for you and reassure yourself (if there was ever any doubt) that you made the right investment with your iPad.*

HOW CAN THE iPAD HELP ME TAKE CARE OF BUSINESS?

Discovering apps that enhance the business side of your studio may be a place for you to begin using your iPad. You could then move into using the iPad more at lessons when your confidence increases. The Apple Store's name for business apps is "Productivity". Here are some apps I highly recommend or have reviewed or use regularly that could prove essential to your business/productivity.

THE APPS LISTED BELOW WILL TURN YOUR iPAD INTO A...

CLOSET IN THE CLOUD

Dropbox - *2GB Free with 500MB Free for Every Referral*

GB stands for gigabyte which stands for multiple units of bytes. To be exact: one gigabyte is 1,000,000,000 bytes. Not enough room to store that many shoes, but enough storage space for a good number of documents and pics and such. MB stands for megabyte or 1,000,000 bytes (obviously not as big of storage space).

The founder of Dropbox, Drew Houston, was tired of keeping track of his USB flash drive and therefore designed an app that allows users to store and share files, access the files from any other device and invite others to see them as well. This is a free service (with limited storage) that lets you access all your photos, docs, and videos anywhere. Although there are other cloud services, the Dropbox app was perhaps the first of its kind to simplify the task of viewing and sharing files specifically on the iPad. (FYI: this app can be accessed online and is not housed soley on your iPad.)

Time for a closer look.

Committee Work: When asked to be part of a committee to plan a national conference, Bradley Sowash, the Chair, suggested opening a Dropbox account on our computers so we could share documents. This allowed each of us to not only view them but also edit with ease - no back and forth emailing, etc. We are each notified if one of us adds or modifies a file with a small note from the Dropbox icon at the top of the computer screen. The beauty of the Dropbox app? All of these documents, pictures, etc. can be viewed on my iPad and iPhone as well - indispensable when on the go.

Document Preservation: For my masters degree, I wrote a thesis on Lynn Freeman Olson, a treasured pedagogue in the world of piano teaching. For research purposes, I held phone conversations with his colleagues including Barbara Kreader. When working on the Music Teachers National Association (MTNA) conference mentioned above, I emailed Barbara to ask if she would be a participant. Although I was not sure if she would remember me from my grad school days and our brief conversation, she did and then even asked to read my thesis. After recovering from the fact that there was interest in my scholarly work of bygone years, I rushed to my basement storage room and retrieved my one and only hard copy of the 200+ page document. After scanning it, the entire paper has found a home in my Dropbox, which I then shared with Barbara. Dropbox created a link to the thesis and I could send this link via email to her, and the bonus: I have access to it on my iPad. It has been so satisfying to reread my work of years ago that previously sat collecting dust in the basement. This event prompted me to take swift action with this academic "hoop" that consumed me for two years. It has been safely preserved in Dropbox storage - whew...come flood or fire to the basement, the thesis would have been gone forever.

Sharing Photos: I wanted to send out photos of a summer studio camp to my piano student families. Within minutes, I moved a number of photos to Dropbox, which then created a link to the "gallery" of photos. I included the link in my latest studio newsletter. What a breeze.

Backup Plan: If you've had your computer stolen (yes, I did) then Dropbox is a security blanket you won't want to live without. Storing files here guarantees accessibility from any computer, not just your own. They can never be stolen. In addition, if your computer or iPad is damaged or goes missing, your Dropbox will not crash and nothing will be lost, except the money spent on replacing your device.

There ARE other storage options beyond Dropbox. I use these other cloud storage devices in ways similar to the examples above. Another one of my favorite apps right now is Google Drive. Perhaps the biggest reason to have more than one storage app is the fact that each one offers limited "shelf space" with an option to purchase more room. Dropbox offers less free space, although you can earn more free space by referring the app to others. Google Drive is more generous with storage space when you sign up and charges less if you need more room. They both have their pros and cons, just make sure you have at least one!

PAPERLESS NOTE PAD

Evernote - *Free/Upgrades Available*

The New York Times declares this app as one of the "Top 10 Must-Have Apps." Being one that does not want to miss out, I immediately downloaded the app. Honestly, my favorite part of this app is the ability to make as many lists as I want with the option to create small check boxes. It brings me great joy when anything on my list earns a check mark! But, there is SO much more to this app. It keeps notes organized, captures any ideas from the web, allows you to access them on any device and helps you find all this stuff fast.

I recently discovered how handy this app is for lesson assignments. As I type out lesson notes during the lesson to be emailed to my students afterwards, Evernote provides an organized format in which to store and tag notes. With their web clipping option I can find and "clip" the perfect worksheet I need for a student and place it in the student's notebook for easy retrieval at the lesson. While working with an adult student playing by ear, I recorded my "improv" on a chord progression in Evernote and it was emailed to the student's inbox where he could listen to the recording on his iPad.

LIBRARY A FINGER TIP AWAY

Kindle - *Free*

Even though Amazon created its own tablet for reading books, you can still download the Kindle App and read any book in the Kindle eBook collection along with those at the iTunes store. iBooks is a built-in app on the iPad; however, only books from the iBook store can be purchased for download in the iBook app.

Some favorite reasons for reading digital editions on the iPad:

- Although the price of an iPad is substantially more than a Kindle or "Nook", the versatility of the iPad and its ability to turn itself into a Nook or Kindle with a tiny app AND so much more makes the iPad worth the purchase.
- Favorite quotes can be highlighted with ease by tapping and dragging along sentences.
- By holding my finger on any word that I don't understand, a definition will pop up on the bottom.
- The virtual shelves of my reader apps have a great deal more space than my physical studio shelves. I really don't want to accumulate that many more print books. That being said, sometimes there is nothing better than the smell, the feel and the touch of a beautifully bound book. So I tend to purchase some of both digital and print.
- When reading in bed, the iPad screen is lit and can be read in the dark so if I start dozing, I don't have to lean over and turn off the lamp.

BANK TELLER

 Square - *Free but %2.75 per swipe*

The next time a family is late with a payment and claims they'll bring it to the next lesson because they forgot the checkbook, you can happily say: "I accept credit cards!" Simply download the app, and a free card reader will be mailed to you. Once you link your bank account, you plug in the card reader and begin swiping. It's a great addition to any studio "store front"!

SCANNER

 Turbo Scan - *$1.99*

I must confess, this one is on my phone but I use it all the time and wanted to include it in here. If you are like me, I often forget to write down who has borrowed a book or who just received a new book for purchase. Now I track books by turbo-scanning them with my iDevice. Simply type in the student's name and price of the book to be purchased or loaned. Delete the scan once the fee is entered into your records or when the book is returned.

8 IT'S OFFICI̶̶̶REE HUGGER

IS THERE A WAY TO AVOID A PAPER TRAIL?

An immediate benefit of owning an iPad is an unemployed printer. As most paper worksheets, forms, etc. eventually land in the trash can, the iPad can eliminate the waste, save on ink expenses and keep documents organized.

SAVE-A-TREE WORKSHEETS

Notability - *$2.99*

In 2012, Apple listed Notability as the bestselling note-taking app of 2012. Having no idea of Notability's celebrity status, I simply purchased the app because someone had recommended it. Now I find myself staying awake at night figuring out new ways to use this productivity app to its full potential. It has and will continue to change how I organize worksheets or theory tests for my students.

Notability integrates handwriting, PDF annotation, typing, recording, and organizing all in one place. These features caught my eye immediately because it gave me the ability to:

1 Download, view and annotate any PDF worksheets, important documents, etc.
2 Organize the worksheets as I please.

To maintain a certain amount of accountability for my students' theory knowledge (which, in my opinion, is most effectively taught at the keys during lessons with reinforcement at lab time), I decided it would be good for my students to take the Colorado State Music Teacher Association (CSMTA) Practice Theory Tests and see how many levels they could pass. This would help me determine what to assign next during lab time and to cover gaps in comprehension. The tests include 12 levels totaling 32 pages. Uggh..I did not want to print out 40 some copies for my students.

So I...
- Created a file "subject" called CSMTA Theory Tests in Notability
- Accessed the tests online on the iPad via Safari, its built in web browser

- Clicked on the link and la
- After tapping on the scre ... ing "Open in iBooks" and another appearred "Open In", allo
- After tapping on "Open I
- Tapped on Notability and
- Tapped on "Create a Ne
- Immediately this placed ... Theory Tests."

Once the test was securely in its place, it was easy to make copies in Notability. By tapping and holding my finger on the file, the word "Duplicate" appeared. Tapping on "Duplicate" made a new copy magically appear. Tapping on the "Edit" button on the top left allows the file name to be changed. I added a student's name to the copied document. To exit the "Edit" mode I clicked "Done." I did this for every student.

Here's where things get REALLY nifty. In Notability you can create "Categories," which look like file folders, and "Subjects", which appear like file headings that can be color-coded easily. So I created a "Category" titled "Students" and then beneath that created a "subject" file for each student family. I color-coded these files according to the days the students arrive for lessons so I can find them easily. (OK, just about finished.) Then I moved a copy of the CSMTA theory tests, which included the students' name, in the appropriately named file folder.

I know, this sounds like a great deal of work but really, once I figured out the system, it was easy. It has worked like a charm and NO one complained about taking the tests on the iPad as they can choose their ink color and zoom in to answer any questions. I saved a tree and now I have a record of these tests, organized and easily accessed. The tests can also be taken again thanks to the ease with which you can annotate and also erase on Pdfs.

ONLINE TEACHING RESOURCES

If you are like me, you're always looking for the perfect worksheet and more often than not, they can be found at a number of well-known blogs/websites. Even better, when you can combine a couple of resources, you can create a fine learning opportunity for students.

Here's how I use Wendy Steven's Web Rewards with Notability. First, an explanation from Wendy Stevens, ComposeCreate.com, about her Web Rewards:

Web Rewards is a free, comprehensive service provided by ComposeCreate.com to help you assist your students as they prepare for Music Progressions and other state theory and listening tests (especially Kansas, Washington State, and North Idaho). As a teacher, you can use the online activities in your own lab or encourage your students to complete the activities at home online. Included in this service are free Melodic and Rhythmic Dictation exercises that are difficult to find. Worksheets, online games and other preparatory activities are also included.[1]

---

[1] Wendy Stevens, Web Rewards, http://www.composecreate.com/web-rewards/ (May 2012).

Although eager to integrate this program into my curriculum, I was not excited about printing off the downloadable worksheets included in each level as I'm really trying to avoid using paper when possible. Enter the Notability app. So I created a Web Rewards "Category" and then created a "Subject" for each level of Web Rewards. By visiting ComposeCreate.com, I was able to download all the worksheets of Level One in the Level One Subject file. I then continued to do this for each level.

During my studio's lab time, students are assigned a Web Reward level. In each level, there are several times where the course asks students to download and complete a worksheet. Instead of downloading the sheet, students duplicate the correct worksheet within the Notability app. Once it is duplicated, students edit the title, adding their name behind the title of the worksheet. After their lesson, I move the completed worksheet to the student's personal file. FYI: my students have become completely comfortable with maneuvering through this app and are eager to "file" their worksheets into their own file themselves.

Each level of Web Rewards features systematically collected exercises from various websites to correlate with concepts. Some of the assigned games in the Web Rewards are accessible on the iPad. So far, I have had success with drills found at MusicTheory.net, and MusicLearningCommunity.com and Teoria. For example, if you access Web Rewards on the iPad and tap on any MusicTheory.net exercise, there is a prompt asking if you wish to "Open the exercise in Tenuto" (an app for the mobile devices), "View Tenuto in the App Store" or "Use the web version." Some exercises from other sites are not accessible on the iPad due to the fact that the iPad does not have Adobe Flashplayer.

Web Rewards includes excellent ear training examples; however, it is tough for students to write their answers on the worksheet that is stored in Notability while listening to the exercises on the iPad. So, if you choose not to print out the worksheets and use the iPad and Notability for the written work, you may want your students to complete these ear training exercises with the computer. That being said, it really is possible to do almost everything else required of the Web Rewards on the iPad. Oh, and don't forget to purchase the Web Rewards Answer Key and Checklists. With the checklist, students mark off what they accomplish as they each have a copy of the checklist in their Notability file. To check my students' work, I open the answer key on my computer and compare student answers on the iPad--no paper trail!

Now is as good of time as ever to chat about the Tenuto app. Here's how the makers describe it:

"Tenuto is a collection of 13 customizable exercises designed to enhance your musicality. From recognizing chords on a keyboard to identifying intervals by ear, it has an exercise for you. Tenuto also includes five musical calculators for accidentals, intervals, chords, analysis symbols, and twelve-tone matrices."

I see it as an in-depth, versatile resource that provides no-frill drills. This is definitely a lifetime app and one to recommend to your students as they build their theory skills for AP and college courses. With the ease it is to use the app with Wendy's Web Rewards, this is a small investment with big payoffs.

PDF'S

As the world of self-publishing grows exponentially, there is no better place to store and view a recently purchased Pdf than your iPad. Once you download a document, tap on the document on the screen and you will be prompted to choose an app in which to open and store it. iBooks, Notability, Kindle, Evernote, just to name a few, all provide excellent ways to organize your purchase (and annotate them, too).

Examples: If you are looking for clear instructions on interpreting chord symbols, Bradley Sowash created a Pdf doc called *Understanding Chord Symbols* with large visuals. They are perfectly sized for easy reference during lessons. Similarly, Wendy Steven's *Rhythm Menagerie* and *Rhythm Manipulations* are large, downloadable books that teach rhythms. They can be downloaded and viewed easily on the iPad - handy if you don't need to make multiple copies.

MUSIC SCORES

Musicians of all kinds of genres and occupations find storing and viewing music scores on the iPad an indispensable option. Read more about score readers in Chapter 9. The verdict? Still out in my mind as page turns are still tricky and staves are small. Although I can see quite well, I find my glasses come in handy more often than not (ughhh). So my question is: who needs an iPad Mini? I can't wait for the release of the iPad maxi!

VIDEO QR ▶

9 POWER TOOLS TO EMPOWER YOUR TEACHING

HOW CAN THE iPAD BE USED DURING LESSONS?

Consider your iPad not just a tool, but a power tool. With the help of innovative developers, there is no limit to the capabilities of this little-over-a-pound device.

With this transformative power, I find myself using the iPad during just about every lesson because it can morph into a:

METRONOME

 Steinway Metronome - *Free*

I require all student families to secure a metronome, but they do not always heed my instructions. Now, with the availability of free metronome apps, physical metronomes have become a moot point (ahh..we really do like our freebies, don't we). Because of its relative ease of use, I usually recommend *Steinway's* metronome app. The app is (as with most) available for more devices than just the iPad. Of course you can also purchase metronome apps that may be better and offer more features (*free - $1.99 or more*). In the end, I'm just happy my students have some kind of metronome in hand.

SCORE READER

 forScore - *$6.99*

The top score reader or sheet music viewer for the iPad appears to be forScore. I don't use this power tool as much as I would like but I know I will grow more accustomed to doing so in the future. Recently, I played at a memorial service only bringing my iPad with Pdfs of the sheet music loaded into forScore. It felt strange having no physical sheet music but all worked well and I left the service with no paper trail. Essentially any Pdf can be read on the iPad. Score readers such as forScore allow you to read, turn pages and

even mark and highlight the score. Some apps even record you as you play and feature a metronome. As I encourage students to learn the latest pop tunes, I often buy scores from Musicnotes.com. Most of my purchased downloads are automatically synced to my iPad. I usually print off a copy for my students, but it is nice to have a copy of it on the iPad for viewing at the lesson.

One more thing: to my delight, I have found a blue-tooth-operated foot pedal remarkably handy for turning pages while playing from a score on the iPad. Read more about that fabulous accessory in Chapter 11.

LEAD SHEET GENERATOR

iReal b - *$7.99 with In-App Purchases Available*
Thanks to my good friend and colleague, Bradley Sowash, I was introduced to iReal b. The app allows you to create chord charts.

Here's Bradley's description on how he uses the app:

Q: How do you use the iReal b app with your students?
A: I use iReal b to create rhythm section backing tracks for my students' current scale/chord drill of the week. I also strongly urge them to practice their pop/jazz repertory with it (there are hundreds of free pre-made tracks on the users forum).

Q: What are the benefits?
A: It is so much more fun (and addictive) to practice to a drum machine or rhythm section than to a metronome. I can tell immediately when a student has actually practiced with iReal b because their beat is steady, the groove is deeper and their confidence shows.

Q: Do you have students purchase the app too?
A: Yes, it's $7.99. There are also in-app purchases of additional style packs for the same price but they aren't necessary for student work. Not all of my students use it but I wish they would.

Q: Anything else you wish to add?
A: This app serves the same function as Band in a Box, which I've used for years. With BIAB, I sent home MIDI files so they could practice with their computer and I still use BIAB for students who are not app-capable. However, I prefer that they use iReal b because the tempo and groove are adjustable on their end. This app is cheaper and does not include some of the features of Band in a Box but students don't need all the extra functionality of BIAB anyway.

SLOWDOWNER

While I was attending a workshop about the latest tech gadgets for musicians, one item was showcased that slowed down any iTunes or CD track. As I usually feel the need to fidget during presentations such as this, I wondered if there might be an app that would do the same thing. My web quest on my iPad took me to Anytune. My apologies to the presenter as the rest of the hour I was engaged in downloading and learning all about this app.

 Anytune - *$14.99*

This is invaluable to me as a pianist and a teacher of those who enjoy playing pop music. Many times, sheet music is not available or the arrangement is not as close to the original as a pianist would like. This app slows down any tune in a device's iTunes library - just one of the many favorite features of this power tool.

The app also can change the pitch of any tune. This can be incredibly helpful, especially for a rookie. For example, if a student wants to learn a favorite popular tune by ear but is most comfortable playing it on the white keys, the tune can be imported from the iTunes library to Anytune. If the original key is not C or A minor, with a quick tap on the plus or minus button, the tune can be transposed up or down to match the student's key preference. The app provides all the benefits of playing with a "band" without the hassle of working around all those tricky black keys.

RECORDING STUDIO AND MORE

 Garage Band - *$4.99*

This extraordinary software program has been modified as an iPad app. I'm still unraveling how best to implement this power-packed app for use in lessons and lab assignments. Here are just a few possibilities I've uncovered so far:

- **Smart Drums:** Some students benefit much more playing with a full drum section to dictate the steady beat vs the drone of a metronome. With the Smart Drum instrument option, you can create a rockin' back beat within seconds to suit a current student piece. This can be recorded, looped and edited as much as you like. Once the back track is created as you wish, it can be sent to your iTunes library or emailed. Students can enjoy playing along with their custom-made back track at home.

- **Smart Instruments:** The patterns supplied with a single tap provide an overwhelming palette full of colors with which to create spectacular tracks. Won't go into details here, but seeing how easily outstanding sounds can be generated by the Garage Band app, I foresee a fabulous creative assignment for my budding composers/arrangers.

- **Audio Recorder:** Using either the iPad microphone or an external microphone connected to your device (learn more in Chapter 11), your iPad brings a recording studio to your home, no traveling necessary. If the sound is not to your liking, there are plenty of ways to tweak or equalize it until it pleases you. Of course, the recording can be sent directly to iTunes to share with friends and neighbors.

LESSON NOTE BINDER

Moosic Studio - *$39.99*

Wow, sometimes I wish I could start all over. Well, that may be an overstatement, but there's something about the tools offered to piano teachers now a days that are so nifty and savvy. Not surprising that I would say something like this as you know I'm a huge fan of iPad apps (duh) and any tech tool that enhances my teaching style. If I was forced to begin again, I'd be highly interested in using a recently released iPad app called Moosic Studio to keep my studio in order.

What intrigues me the most about Moosic Studio is the fact that this app was developed by a husband for his wife, a piano teacher. No one is aligned to the daily woes and needs of a piano teacher more than a spouse. Can you imagine the luxury of having someone in-house who listens and builds a product to suit your personal studio needs? Once you take a look inside the app, you'll see that this teacher married well :-).

Usually I like to write about apps that I've experienced first hand, but I must admit, I have not yet employed the app to its full potential. I already have a system in place for scheduling, etc and because of time constraints, I can't foresee changing over to this system right now. That being said, for any of you who are launching a studio, looking for a way to streamline lesson scheduling or desperate for a means to organize your studio with the ease of an iPad, here's a fine solution.

Instead of providing a general outline of the app's features, let me zero in on a favorite. As I make it a point to follow-up lessons by emailing lesson notes, I was particularly interested in seeing how Moosic Studio provides lesson feedback. I was pleased to find a fabulous system obviously custom-made for piano teachers. Once student general information has been entered, tapping on the individual's name will lead to a screen where a great deal more information can be stored for that particular pianist. One category is labeled Assignment History. Selecting this option will take you to an array of additional category titles with sub menus.

- Lesson Dates of all past lessons
- Attendance: On Time, Late, No Show
- Books: Brought Books, Did Not Bring Books
- Lesson Event/Performance: Outstanding, Good, Needs Improvement
- Teacher Comments (not shared with students)
- Lesson/Event Notes
- Circle of 5ths: Hands (together, separately), Pentascales, Tetrascales, Scales, etc...
- Assignments: Add Book Assignment, Sight Reading, Apps/Online, Notes
- Attach Media: Audio Recordings, Video Recordings, Timed Events

All of these items can be selected and completed during the lesson. There is ample space to write comments and yes, even make video and audio recordings that can be shared with a student via Dropbox and other apps. However, the most extraordinary portion of the app is that all these menu items mentioned above are neatly organized into a lovely template that can be:

- Printed at the lesson
- Opened in another app such as Dropbox, Kindle, Notability, forScore, iBooks, Evernote, Google Drive
- Emailed directly to the student.

Oh my, I've been looking for something like this that totes versatility and ease of communication with student families and finally found it!

From my conversations with Carlos Fontiveros, the developer, it is clear he is continually updating Moosic Studio and adding new features to piano teachers' wish list.

This description uncovered a small portion of what this powerhouse app offers. In addition, it seems Moosic Studio will have strong support from the developer. I imagine there is pressure to please as his number one customer lives in the same house. To get the full scoop check out the app website www. moosicstudio.com for a rundown of all the features.

With heftier price tags, these apps are heavy hitters and are packed with potential. They could prove intimidating and the learning curve steep but DON'T miss out. They are worth the climb.

"[A] breadth of offering [in your instruction]...means that if students are starting to grow weary of a studio activity they're currently enrolled in, they can switch to another activity and still stay in your studio. This gives you a huge advantage over the "Static" studios that offer traditional weekly lessons only: the only way their students can meaningfully change what they're doing is to leave." -Philip Johnston[2]

---

[2] Philip Johnston, *The Dynamic Studio: How to Keep Students, Dazzle Parents and Build the Music Studio Everyone Wants to Get Into* (Philip Johnston, 2012), 57.

OTHER APPS THAT FALL INTO THIS HEAVY-DUTY CATEGORY INCLUDE:

 Home Concert Xtreme - *$39.99*

 iMovie - *$4.99*

 Keynote - *$9.99*

 NoteStar - *Free*

and more...

I could go on and on. This brief chapter barely scrapes the surface of the power tool apps available for your iPad that are capable of igniting every lesson. Imagine what the future holds.

VIDEO QR ▶

10 WELCOME TO YOUR STUDIO ARCADE

DISCLAIMER: *Due to the constant changes in the world of technology, what you are about to read is not anywhere close to being complete or up to date. If I really like an app, I write about how I use it in my column, "One App at a Time" at 88PianoKeys.me. It is my intent that this collection of "stories" about my app experiences will spur you to explore individual apps yourself. This will help you secure the apps that work for you and reassure yourself (if there was ever any doubt) that you made the right investment with your iPad.*

HOW MANY WAYS CAN THE iPAD BE USED DURING *LAB* TIME?

The answer to this question: infinite. Instead of overwhelming you, I'll provide three examples that illustrate how the iPad can be invaluable as a teaching assistant. Some apps even pose as arcade-like games – maybe not quite as enthralling as the pinball, ball toss or shooting galleries of years past, but certainly more fun and interactive than flash cards or a theory book.

USE THE iPAD TO NAME NOTES

 Flashnote Derby - *$0.99*    **Note Squish** - *$0.99*

One app investigation began by assigning my students to play note name drills using the Flashnote Derby app. A couple of weeks before, they had enjoyed using the Note Squish app. These are two similar apps that offer a unique venue to master note recognition. Really, both are nothing more than ordinary flash cards but are much more fun than sifting through cards because of the rich graphics, the game format and of course the best part: they are played on the iPad.

In my studio I made a large investment in a magnetic white board (*note: it was pricey because of the added staff lines.*) On the board, I created a voting system - voters placed a magnet beneath their favorite app title. Flashnote Derby took the crown over Note Squish. Students explained that Note Squish was harder to read because the answers "jumped around" and they liked the racing screen better than the arcade style graphics of Note Squish. However, some were extremely loyal to Note Squish and adamant it was the "winner."

I like Flashnote Derby because it provides...

- Instructional videos of each portion of the grand staff; therefore it teaches as well as provides drills
- The ability to isolate line-note names or space-note names (even as little as 2 notes)
- The option to isolate note names on the treble clef, bass clef or both.

I like Notes Squish because it allows for...

- The option to choose between treble, bass OR alto clef (but not a combination of treble and bass)
- Drills that include as little as two note names
- Just plain fun - the graphics are adorable.

USE THE iPAD TO TACKLE THEORY

 Octavian Basics - *$2.99*

When preparing for a recital and focusing so much on one piece, the time is ripe to not only memorize the key of the piece but also master its scales and chords AND know how to spell and notate both. However, with limited lesson time, my introduction of these important theory concepts needs to be packed with memorable, hands-on experiences. I ask students to "listen first before they look" with as many of these concepts as time allows.

A while ago, Susan Paradis, an incredibly imaginative teacher and blogger who offers countless teaching ideas, provided beautiful templates for "W" and "H" cards at her website. She suggested using pencil eraser replacements to identify the keys to use in a scale. The students measure the distance between each [piano] key and label it with a "W" card for whole or "H" card for half step. I took it one step further and wrote numbers [corresponding with scale degrees] on the erasers. As I believe it is crucial for students to see and memorize where half-steps occur within a scale, this process provides the perfect visual for what makes a major scale (half steps between scale degrees 3,4 and 7,8) or a minor scale (half steps between 2,3 and 5,6). Students are asked to memorize these codes (ex: 34-78) - just as permanently as their zip code.

Once the scale is constructed and fingering refined, there is nothing like the Octavian Basics app as it displays the scale and also the diatonic chords, chord symbols, inversions and even the intervals found in each scale (and more)! Although I thoroughly enjoy introducing these concepts myself, the app encompasses the basic elements through powerful visual and aural experiences, which greatly enhances student comprehension.

Along with Octavian Basics, the student pianist and I review a sheet I created (All About Scales) to be completed during lab time.

The worksheet asks theory enthusiasts to:

- Identify the key signature from the circle of keys
- Circle the key and the mode
- Place either a white or blue sticker on the 8 scale degrees (white stickers representing white keys and

blue for black - can't find black stickers!)
- Notate the scale
- Notate the three primary chords in root, 1st and 2nd inversions
- Notate the diatonic chords and label with chords symbols and Roman numerals
- Notate the intervals found in the scale.

On the sheet, the three primary scale degrees and chords are color coded with the three primary colors, matching my bulletin board hanging by the piano. Blue = Tonic, Yellow = Subdominant and Red = Dominant. Comparing primary chords to primary colors helps students understand the importance of those three chords and why I drill them over and over and over.

If you are wondering, yes, my students "cheat" and use Octavian to help them complete the worksheet. They use head phones so they can listen to all the elements they are constructing. The point of completing the sheet is not a test of knowledge; instead, it is a chance to learn terms, learn how to notate and become familiar with a good dose of theory. Quizzes and tests can come later. Also, my early level students complete only the sections I assign. The sheets are always saved in the students' binders. Concepts can always be referenced or completed later as their theory knowledge grows. As students prepare new repertoire, they will complete a sheet for each piece (and new key) and acquire a collection of valuable key information (pun intended) in their binder for future reference.

Octavian Basics offers a number of other features including solfege (do, re, mi... syllables) and additional scales and modes. Once your theory experts outgrow this app, make sure to have the Octavian Keyboard Calculator (the big bro) on hand. This app features an extraordinary amount of scales, chords and progressions above and beyond the Octavian Basics, all provided in 5 different languages.

USE THE iPAD TO REVIEW RHYTHMS

Why is it that reading rhythms and taking rhythmic dictation are such difficult tasks? I won't go into detail now, but I have my theories. Since most students need a couple of booster shots worth of rhythmic review, it's important to have a number of apps on hand that drill this essential music element. At first, I had a hard time tracking down apps that drill rhythmic concepts, but recently I found two that have become my favorites.

 Rhythm Lab - *$1.99*

Rhythm Lab provides ample excerpts of leveled rhythm exercises that students must tap in one hand or two, keeping in time with a metronome. Players are graded on their accuracy. The vast array of rhythms would keep most rhythmic aficionados busy and challenged for days.

MyRhythm - *$1.99*

An excellent counter part to Rhythm Lab is My Rhythm. I immediately grabbed this app when designing a pop music unit for my studio. The gist? Instead of focusing on reading the intricate note value symbols, players must follow a grid of dots and play the patterns with both hands on drum pads. With a menu of groove styles and a library of hip sounds for each hand, this app encourages students to read non-traditional rhythm symbols and coordinate the tricky rhythms between the hands while feeling the groove - perfect for the keeping the pulse of pop music.

♪ *There are countless apps and more appear daily. Because of this, I'm guessing that some apps may have a short shelf life due to lack of popularity and as a result of loss of developer support. I'm crossing my fingers that doesn't happen to my favorites but it may happen. To keep my stash of apps armed and ready for lab assignments, I keep a growing app collection. My "stockroom of apps" helps me be prepared with a quick fix when I need that perfect app for "slow-reader Suzy" or "term-challenged Timmy" or "lack-luster-listening-skills Louise." As students use the various apps, we all begin to compare and determine the "cream of the crop." There's not a better place in which to conduct this type of research than within my own studio with my faithful and opinionated students. My lab: the "app Petri dish."*

11 IT'S ALL IN THE ACCESSORIES

I've always been a fan of accessories so perhaps that's why I felt it necessary to include this chapter.

ONCE I PURCHASE AN iPAD AND APPS, WILL I NEED ANYTHING ELSE?

That favorite scarf, killer shoes or a piece of bling may be the perfect compliment to an outfit but are admittedly not necessary. In the same way, the accessories listed below are not required for you to take advantage of your iPad, but once you purchase any or all of them, you may wonder how you survived (dressed) without them.

Stylus - *$.50+*

With so many students using my iPad there's something especially pleasant about not having all their fingers touching my screen.

I've never regretted this addition to my studio: a wall-mounted hand sanitizer dispenser. It cost less than $20, included refills for a year and was worth every penny.

A stylus is a fancy name for a stick with a soft tip on the end used to tap on the iPad screen. I have yet to buy an expensive stylus ($20 or more) just because they are small and can be easily lost. Instead, I buy inexpensive ones through Amazon that run about 50 cents a piece.

RCA cord - *around $10*

Some years ago, my "iLife" changed forever. I enjoyed using an iPod but did not see a use for it in the studio on a daily basis. Thanks to a conference session led by Serena Mackey, I learned how to hook up my iPod and, of course, later my iPad to my Clavinova CVP-505. I make it a habit to download all of my CD's to my iTunes library and sync them with my iPad. The RCA cord provides a connection between the iPad and Clavinova that serves as an amazing sound system. When students and I go shopping for the next repertoire piece, tunes are literally at my fingertips and readily available for browsing. With the growing accumulation of apps such as iReal b, Steinway Metronome and of course YouTube, which can all be enhanced by a ample speakers, this iPad accessory is enjoyed on a daily basis.

What do you need? An RCA cord. The 1/4 inch adaptors on one end of the cord connect to the auxiliary IN and OUT found beneath the Clavinova cabinet. Yep, I need to lie on the floor to connect these correctly as they are hard to find without looking. However, it is worth the effort as the 1/8 inch stereo adaptor on the other end plugs easily into any iDevice. You couldn't ask for a better sound system.

♪ *Thanks to an adult student who bought my old Clavinova, he discovered that borrowing the mp3 cord used in his car to connect an iPhone to the car stereo system could also connect an iAnything to the Clavinova with the help of an adaptor. Note: this is a different adaptor (male) than the others used above--did you know adaptors have genders? OK maybe you did, but I learned something new. Remember, I'm a high-achieving consumer and not a tech expert.*

There is not a day that I don't use the benefits of this RCA cord accessory. Why not make your Clavinova or digital keyboard an "iKeyboard"?

Camera Connection Kit - $29

I've been a fan of a score-following software program called Home Concert Xtreme (HCX) for quite some time and it is now available as an iPad app. FYI: "when used with a MIDI keyboard, HCX Play-Along Apps respond to your playing by following your timing, tempo, and volume, giving you your own accompanist, rehearsal tool, and music tutor."[1] When I learned HCX was available as an iPad app, I immediately bought it. However, I discovered that because this app must connect to a MIDI keyboard, the power-tool app needs an accessory called the Camera Connection Kit. As previously stated, tech lingo is not my thing so for an explanation, I've gone directly to the source (and the developer of Home Concert Xtreme), George Litterst - well-known for his music tech expertise - for the most accurate description of why this kit is a necessity.

"To connect a MIDI keyboard to an iOS device using a USB cable, you'll need Apple's *Camera Connection Kit Adapter* (for devices with the dock connector) or Apple's *Lightning-to-USB Camera Adapter* (for the newer iOS devices)...These adapters turn your mobile device's dock or Lightning port into a USB port (like the one on your computer). This solution will work with most MIDI keyboards that have a USB option. NOTE: These USB camera adapter solutions work with the iPad but do not work with iPhone and iPod touch. The iConnect MIDI interface, however, will work with the iPhone and iPod touch."[2]

Take George's advice - this works well - and now my iPad is "MIDI-ed up" and talking nicely to my Clavinova.

Page Flip Pedal - *starting at $89.95*

The savvy Jennifer Foxx blogs regularly about how she uses technology, the iPad and apps in her studio at http://fpsresources.wordpress.com/. After reading Jennifer's "testimony" of how much she "loved" her *PageFlip Cicada* pedal (read all about her love affair here)[3] I was immediately envious of her newfound accessory and had to purchase one myself. So I did, and then it

[1] Zenph, *iPad Apps*, http://www.zenph.com/zenph-software/ipad, (May 2013). [2] George Litterst, *Connecting a MIDI Keyboard with an iPad or Other iOS Device*, http://www.claviercompanion.com/connect/blog/50-connect-midi-keyboard-to-ipad, (January 2013). [3] Jennifer Foxx, *Tech Tuesday Hands Free Pedal for iPad*, http://fpsresources.wordpress.com/2012/07/25/tech-tuesday-hands-free-pedal-for-ipad/, (July 2012).

sat there, in its box ready to be opened, used and loved. There's a clinical mindset called "approach avoidance" and I had a good case of this condition with the unopened box. I feared that once opened, the instructions to use it would be daunting, things wouldn't work even if it was supposed to be simple, and it would take much longer than I was willing to spend to get it up and running. To my complete delight, the pedal was working within minutes thanks to the blue tooth capabilities of the iPad and this slick page-turning pedal. Although there is a learning curve to get the foot turning pages for you instead of your hand, it didn't take me long to catch on and enjoy the luxury of hands free page turning.

Blue Snowball Mic - *around $100*

Currently, this accessory is on my list thanks to PianoAnne's inspiring blog about her experience. PianoAnne, aka Anne Crosby, at http://pianoanne.blogspot.com/ is another blogger with creative teaching ideas and excellent advice when it comes to using technology. She claims all you need is the USB adapter from the Apple iPad *Camera Connection Kit* to hook this mic up to your iPad. Piano Anne used the Voice Memos for iPad app and states:

"[This app] is really simple to use. I can easily keep track of the files and share them by email with iTunes. You can get a little fancier if you want by using the Garageband app."[4]

Once you become involved in the blogging world, it's assumed you will join all the important social media groups such as Facebook, and yes, I have an account and even an 88 Piano Keys page. Although I post on a regular basis, I must confess, I tend to peek in on the conversations of others quite often. I prefer to "like" a comment but avoid posting one as it can stuff my inbox with comment threads. I know, I can unfollow...just a slow learner. However, one, day Leia Sharma[5], a loyal reader of 88 Piano Keys, asked a pertinent question about the Snowball Mic on Kathleen[6] Theisen's group page, Professional Piano Teachers, https://www.facebook.com/groups/professionalpianoteachers/.

Leia posted: "Can anyone recommend a good microphone that I can use to record my students and my own compositions? Ideally, something that can be plugged into my iPad or MacBook. Would appreciate any suggestion!"

I happened to see the question and no one had answered (yet) so I piped in offering the sound advice of PianoAnne and mentioned the Snowball microphone - the one that was still sitting in my Amazon cart (not any more!) and I included the Amazon link. The conversation that followed offered so much helpful information, I asked Kathleen if I could include the thread in my book:

Kathleen: I use that Blue Snowball mic, too. I have a couple of them. If you use it with the iPad, you need the Apple Camera Connector kit to plug in the USB device.

Leia: Thank you for the recommendations!

[4] Anne Crosby Gaudet, *Blue Snowball with the iPad*, http://pianoanne.blogspot.com/2012/05/blue-snowball-with-ipad.html, (May 2012).
[5] Leia Sharma, Teacher. http://www.leiaslessons.com/students.html. [6] Kathleen Theisen, Soprano, Pianist, Teacher, Conductor, Composer. http://www.KathleenTheisen.com.

Kathleen: You can also use a MIDI cable and connect your MIDI piano directly to your computer or iPad and send the sound from the piano to the device as MIDI data, then choose whatever sounds you want within your recording program (like Pro Tools or Garage Band or Finale). Garritan Personal Orchestra comes with some AMAZING digital sample sounds.

Leia: My next question was going to be what app to download to use with it! I don't have any recording apps yet.

Kathleen: It depends on what you want to do. Garage Band is the go-to program for Mac and mobile devices (apple only). Audacity is FREE for Mac and PC. There are many other very high end recording programs that are used by pros and in studios, etc. Most of them run at $400+ and would only be needed if you're multi-tracking and creating your own CDs, etc. Finale and Sibelius are computer programs for composing (notation programs)

Notion and Symphony Pro are iPad APPS for composing (notation programs)

Leia: I have Notion, but I don't think you can record on that?

Kathleen: Notion is for NOTATION. You can 'play' your notes 'into' it.

Leia: Ah, I didn't know you could do that! How cool!

Kathleen: You need the apple camera connector kit to plug in a midi keyboard.

Tim[7]: Apogee MiC is brilliant. High quality and perfect with Mac and iPhone and iPad, and no connection kits required.

Leia: I had heard of Apogee but it's rather pricey! The snowball is half the price!

Kathleen: Snowball is usually about half its own retail price on Amazon or eBay. (It's about $110 in the apple store and about $50-something online)

Tim: Yeah they do cost more but the quality of recording is unsurpassed IMO. Check their website for examples of recordings.

Kathleen Theisen, thank you for letting us eavesdrop on this timely conversation. Everyone's expert advice based on personal experience provided a variety of perspectives and opinions!

---

[7] Tim Topham, Teacher, Performer, Presenter. http://timtopham.com/.

Protective Case/Cover - *$50+*

A necessity! There are some that protect your iPad from any fall. I recommend something sturdy that covers the entire iPad. Confession: both of my iPad covers are black - not my first choice, long story. My advice: make a statement with some color.

Keyboard - *$50-$200*

Visiting family in California is always fun but my most recent stay proved extremely helpful with the addition of my latest accessory. My sister-in-law was given an iPad to use as part of her job (ahhh...must be nice working for the state government!) and I gasped at her cover/keyboard combo. The case includes a blue tooth keyboard and I was stunned by its functionality, versatility and strength. It made the iPad look, feel and function like my lap top. It turns out that my sister-in-law's office had done extensive research on the best case/keyboard combo and the ClamCase took first

place. I had been on the search for the perfect iPad keyboard and found it via the industrious research of others. It was clear I needed one immediately. The only draw back: the cost. Because I didn't spend much on my other covers and because this cover will work with all iPad models (1-4) and because I own no pets - bad excuse - I splurged for the latest aluminum case which runs $169. *Gulp.*

Just like I can never have enough shoes, there will always be more accessories to buy for the iPad. On my growing list: the savvy Apple TV - a wireless wonder that connects all iDevices (and more) to a big screen.

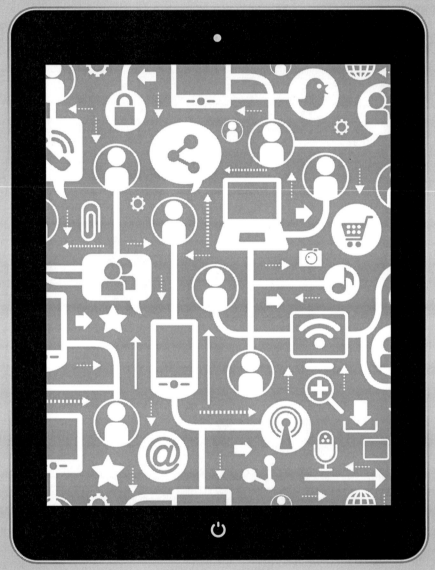

VIDEO QR ▶

12 CONNECTING THE DOTS

IS THERE A CREATIVE SIDE TO THE iPAD?

Remember Steve Jobs' quote in Chapter Two?

> *"Technology alone is not enough. It is technology married with liberal arts, married with the humanities that yields us the results that make our hearts sing."*[1]

When I included that quote, I had no idea how providential it would be. My first intention of this book was to marvel at the wonders of the iPad and technology. It turns out that yes, the iPad is the star of the show but the path that this tool and technology has taken me over the years is the plot of the book. While reflecting upon this path and connecting the dots, it dawned on me that it continues to lead me in one direction: Creativity. The iPad and technology (yes, along with other things, not to mention other people) have shaped my teaching, my experiences, my opportunities, and yes my creativity - the virtue that sets us humans apart or "that makes our hearts sing."[2]

> *"[A tool] is like a finger pointing away to the moon. Don't concentrate on the finger, or you will miss all the heavenly glory."* - Bruce Lee[3]

 Beatwave - *Free*

doodlePad: A gadget for imagination

Remember those short rubbery-coiled phone cords that glued us to our desks? We'd talk tethered to the phone while doodling with a pen on a scratch pad. My guess is some of the best artwork in the house was right there next to the phone, but after hanging up, we walked away and never thought of it again. Cellphones seemed to have erased this pen-and-paper doodling opportunity. But wait, this moment-in-time of no restrictions, to express freely what comes naturally can be achieved again, not by the phone, but on the phone - and iPads, too. The app store is stocked with programs that promote nothing but doodling. Check out Beatwave, Soundrops and Bloom.

Making this connection got me thinking: How could I use these doodling apps for teaching purposes? Does every lab assignment need to be task-driven with strict goals? Why can't I provide a digital sandbox in my studio and promote the art of doodling? Wouldn't this freedom help students overcome their fears of noodling at the keys?

[1] Jonah Lehrer, *Steve Jobs:"Technology Alone is Not Enough"*, http://www.newyorker.com/online/blogs/newsdesk/2011/10/steve-jobs-pixar.html (October 2011). [2] Jonah Lehrer, *Steve Jobs:"Technology Alone is Not Enough"*, http://www.newyorker.com/online/blogs/newsdesk/2011/10/steve-jobs-pixar.html (October 2011). [3] Carl King, *So, You're A Creative Genius (Now What...)* (Michael Wiese Productions, 2011), p54.

Ahh...time to get back to the lab and test this theory! After completing a tough assignment of playing and spelling chords, I asked my lab "assistants" to check out an app called Bubble Harp. I did not explain a thing, just handed them the iPad and headphones. As expected, some students became immediately engaged with the graphics, the sounds and the options while some looked up at me and asked what they were supposed to do. One gal was clearly frustrated as there were no set rules, goals or points to score.

After I explained to her that sometimes it's good to create just for the sake of creating, her sister exclaimed:

"I get it, this is just like why I like to eat cheese so much!"

Enough said. I have no scientific evidence that this type of activity encourages creativity at the keys but it can't hurt.

 Why NOT allow our students and ourselves to create and enjoy the journey, not just the destination?

"With creativity, you've got to jump right into the process and drown in it before you can figure out where you're going." - Carl King[4]

 Notion - *$14.99*

notePad: A device for notation

Yes, it is possible to notate a composition on the iPad. There are a number of programs that offer notation features but the one app I've used is Notion. Without too much trouble, I generated a professional looking score and have dabbled with the option to input notes with a MIDI keyboard as well.

In the summer, I offer options for students, one of them being Composition lessons. A first grader named Ginger eagerly signed up and came to her first lesson with an entire original piece. After some tweaking, we began the process of notating her piece on paper as I wished for her to learn that skill as well. The next lesson she returned and, alas, she had found no time to continue her pencil and paper notation...(nuts!). Knowing that her family owns an iPad and remembering her past uninhibited encounters with the iPad at lessons, I asked her if she wanted to check out Notion with me. The patience she exhibited as we discovered the secrets of the app was amazing. It seems this new generation doesn't mind problem solving and maintains a sense of curiosity over a state of frustration. I learned a great deal from Ginger and wouldn't you know, she left the lesson with a beautifully notated composition in hand. I'll make sure she gets that pencil and paper notation exercise completed next time!

---

[4] Carl King, *So, You're A Creative Genius (Now What...)* (Michael Wiese Productions, 2011), p22. [5] http://techinmusiced.wordpress.com/2013/05/10/latest-notion-update-and-related-thoughts/ May 10 Latest Notion Update and Related Thoughts

Christopher J. Russell, blogger at Technology in Music Education who I regard as an expert in the field of iPad apps, states this about Notion:

"[Notion] offers most of the tools needed by musicians in terms of composition, this is a great bargain. In fact, you can purchase an iPad and Notion for less than the cost of Finale or Sibelius (non-educational version, of course). The only caveat with Notion is to be aware that the app does take up a healthy amount of storage on your iPad at 1.6 GB, much of that sounds (and that is BEFORE the purchase of the additional sounds). If you are running on a 16GB iPad, space may be a consideration."[5]

A while ago, there was a great deal of hype over an app that promised to deliver amazing features. Developers claimed this up-and-coming app would allow users to draw a quarter note with a fingertip and the app would then turn "scribbles" into the correct notation. Apparently the over eager developers did not get the financial support and did not deliver and are now back to the drawing board. Perhaps this group of developers will renew their efforts? They may be worth the time and investment as Russell claims:

"You can create content on an iPad. And apps like Notion for iPad or GarageBand demonstrate that you can do so effectively and even efficiently. Yes, you can use an iPad for content consumption, like any other digital device. But it is foolish in 2013 to say you can't create on the device."[6] -Christopher J Russell

launchingPad: An instrument for innovation
The iPad (along with technology in general) has undoubtedly ignited my teaching style. My fascination with the iPad and blogging about teaching creativity (and teaching creatively) with technology (among other topics) have - to my pleasant surprise - boosted my opportunities to serve with highly respected educators, authors and artists in the field of piano education.

This has been the most difficult chapter to push through, as the thread that holds the following paragraphs to the rest of the book seems thin. However, every time I was tempted to delete them, I felt compelled to keep the paragraphs as they provide a record of the shift in paradigms that is taking place right now in the world of music education. There was firsthand evidence of this at the 2013 Music Teacher's National Association (MTNA) Conference in California at which I was honored to be a presenter and organizer for the Saturday Pedagogy Jazz/Pop track. This shift and my opportunity to experience it firsthand just happened to coincide with my writing this book. My recent experiences seem to be culminating into something bigger than I expected at the onset of this book. So, since it's my book and I decide what happens, bear with me and keep reading.

[6] Christopher J. Russell, *That iPad Isn't Just for Consumption Anymore*, http://techinmusiced.wordpress.com/2013/05/11/that-ipad-isnt-just-for-consumption-anymore/ , (May 2013).

Forrest Kinney's Insights

For a number of centuries, time spent at most piano lessons has been undeniably devoted to interpreting the compositions of famous dead guys: Mozart, Beethoven, Chopin and the like. Forrest Kinney, well known for his *Pattern Play* and *Chord Play* books focusing on improvising and arranging, led a dynamic session as part of the 2013 Music Teachers National Association (MTNA) Jazz/Pop track. He submitted a lovely blog for 88PianoKeys.me highlighting a wonderful backdrop of what it was like before this lopsided focus on interpretation became common practice:

"When Liszt gave the first solo piano recital in 1839, he did not play Beethoven Sonatas or Bach fugues. He only played a few of his own short compositions. Well then, what else did he play? What most performers of the time were playing: arrangements and improvisations. Liszt opened the famous 1839 concert with his arrangement of the William Tell Overture. On his tours, he would see what was playing at the local opera house, and then include a long improvisatory "fantasy" on its themes in that night's concert. He would conclude his concerts with long improvisations on themes suggested by audience members. That had been common practice in concerts for many years. The emphasis in such concerts was on displaying the personal creativity and abilities of the performer, as well as ensuring the enjoyment of the audience.

I often talk about how the future of music education (and in particular, piano instruction) will return to teaching and exploring the four main arts of music: improvising (like talking with tones), arranging (like retelling the stories and themes of the culture), composing (writing essays), and interpreting (reciting and performing scripts). Modern music education is usually focused on one art (interpretation) to the neglect and even exclusion of the others. In the future, pedagogy will encourage piano students to become whole musicians who can freely practice all four arts."[7]

Bradley Sowash's Observations

Bradley Sowash served as chair of the 2013 MTNA Jazz/Pop track and asked me to come alongside him as the project manager thanks to our conversations at prior conferences and my blogs. As a jazz concert artist, composer, educator and author of the number one best-selling jazz method, *That's Jazz*, he has dedicated a great deal of energy promoting well-balanced musicianship at the keys. I was greatly honored to serve with him. After our experience at the conference, he reflected:

"I've been swimming upstream on the subject of teaching creativity as a necessary ingredient to comprehensive musicianship at music teacher meetings all over the country for several years. So it was with particular delight to find that we could attract a packed room of teachers for nine hours of sessions with experts on the subject of teaching popular music styles, improvisation and creativity.

It seems the old model of only teaching the "masters" using only the written page is finally giving way to a more balanced approach or as someone at the conference quipped, "the Queen Mary (of music education) is slowly turning." I can get even more dramatic by declaring, "The eye/ear revolution™ has begun!"[8]

[7] Forrest Kinney, *In Praise of Anderson and Roe*, http://88creativekeys.com/2013/03/19/in-praise-of-anderson-and-roe/, (March 2013).
[8] Bradley Sowash, *The Eye Ear Revolution has Begun*, http://bradleysowash.com/the-eyeear-revoltion-has-begun/, (March 2013).

My Reaction and APPlication

In anticipation of the 2013 MTNA conference opportunity, I began to plan a studio unit around pop music.

 A studio "unit" means that for a number of weeks I plan repertoire and lab events around a certain theme.

Coming back home after my experience working with Bradley Sowash, Forrest Kinney and others at the 2013 MTNA Jazz/Pop track, the point of this "Pop" unit became clearer. It would focus on ways to connect current hit music with that of the past and encourage creativity balancing both eye and ear skills.

 Musicnotes Sheet Music Viewer - *Free*

After I asked for each student's POP 10 list of their favorite tunes, I ordered music books and found some of their requests at MusicNotes.com. Pianists were thrilled to play the songs from their iTunes playlist. Record progress was seen from countless students who normally struggle with practice between lessons. One gal arrived at a lesson and said:

"Just warning you right now, don't expect this much improvement every week."

How does all of this connect to the creative side of the iPad?

This handy device provides innovative teaching opportunities for me to blend current tunes, creativity, ear training drills and yes, even traditions of the past. Let me explain:

1 First, the iPad syncs most songs purchased at MusicNotes.com. Some students were reading the score from their iPad not from a printed page.

2 Students were assigned to search YouTube for a piano cover that inspired them. We watched the videos on the iPad during the lesson for inspiration and creative ideas. Plugging the iPad into my Clavinova (see Chapter 11) provided a fine sound system for listening.

3 Reading rhythms and grooving with the beat is always tricky when playing in contemporary styles so my favorite apps used for building strong rhythmic skills included: Rhythm Lab and MyRhythm as described in Chapter 10.

4 As the pop tune arrangements did not always meet with student "satisfaction," they were encouraged to move beyond the page and create their own piano covers so they also spent time drilling ear skills using an app called Right Note Ear Trainer.

The Orchestra - *$13.99*

5 So back to the "dead guys"...when I asked my students if they could name the most popular current pop singer, there was no consensus, as opinions varied greatly...Mumford and Sons, Fun., Taylor Swift... However, when I asked if they could name great composers from the past, the names Mozart and Beethoven popped up immediately. I thought this was a suitable segue to bring in the old with the new; so, I created a couple of lab assignments dedicated to Beethoven. I stumbled upon a website which offers 20 facts about Beethoven (http://www.classicfm com/composers/beethoven guides/beethoven-20-facts-about-great-composer/last-words/). Students were asked to complete a worksheet (yes, a paper worksheet as these were placed in assignment binders for future reference) to guide them through these facts. Afterwards, the pianists experienced an interactive exploration of Beethoven's 5th Symphony using The Orchestra App. They were mesmerized.

6 At 88pianokeys.me, I offer a Get Inspired! series. Each episode features bios and videos of keyboard artists from various genres meant to inspire budding musicians. I provide a sheet of questions to encourage active listening. Since the questions often include new musical terms such as Allegro, Philharmonic, Baroque, I provide a link to flashcards I created on Quizlet, which can then be viewed on an iPad with an app called Flashcardlet. Here's where the thread continues to build strength! Months before I dreamed up this pop-music-mixed-in-with-some-Beethoven unit, I designed an episode that featured Daniel Barenboim playing Beethoven's Pathetique Sonata and Bradley Sowash playing his original arrangement called "Ellingtoven", which quotes Beethoven's famous tunes: *Ode to Joy, Fur Elise, and 5th Symphony*. Little did I know that my efforts months before would create the perfect wrap up for my studio theme.

Perhaps you find all of this a stretch? So did I, at first. These ideas did not come to me in one planning session - I wish I could say I was that organized. No, they evolved from my 2013 MTNA experience, the insightful observations of my highly esteemed colleagues, recent iPad app discoveries and my need for new weekly lab assignments that fit with my designated unit.

♪ *Although I did not offer a back-up band for my wannabe pop artists at the spring recital as I would have liked, I did offer them a special trophy (as I always do) celebrating their past year of triumphs at the keys. Typical trophies are always appreciated, but for this recital, a Beethoven bust seemed a fitting substitute. This unique trophy served as a token reminder to each of my students that they would continue to be encouraged and equipped "to become whole musicians who can freely practice all four arts."[9]*

keyPad: A key for unlocking creativity

Over 20 years ago, I was inspired by a highly regarded teacher in the area who used a studio lab boasting a computer and ONE software program (back then there was only one available for teaching

[9] Forrest Kinney, *In Praise of Anderson and Roe*, http://88creativekeys.com/2013/03/19/in-praise-of-anderson-and-roe/, (March 2013).

musical concepts). What a difference a decade or two can make. The winding path continues and the plot thickens. The lab and yes, the iPad (the star of the show), have together provided a channel for me to blend tradition with innovation. Although the iPad alone is not the only muse to unlock my creativity as a teacher, it continues to be a key part of my daily lessons and aids me as I carry the torch for the Eye Ear Revolution™.

Since our work together at the 2013 MTNA conference, Bradley Sowash and I are continuing to promote instruction that balances eye and ear skills. Our newest venture, 88 Creative Keys, offers training for students, teachers and pianists of all ages. The program encourages music makers to play beyond the page and make their own brand of music. Yes, we integrate iPad apps into our curriculum! More information about our efforts can be found at EyeEarRevolution.com.

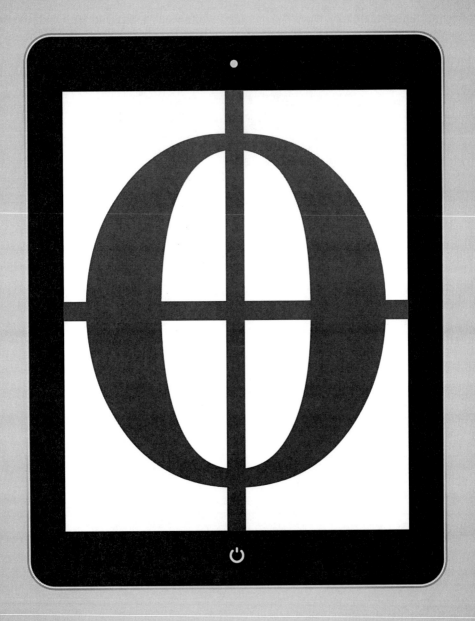

OUTRO

THAT'S IT?

It seems appropriate to place the double bar line of this book at 12 chapters. Twelve is significant because there are musical connections--the 12-tone scale, the12 bar blues--but also because I don't like the number 13. If you made it through each chapter, I hoped that you gained a healthy respect for this handy device called the iPad and realized that yes, I'm a fan of it and like sharing my "obsession" with others. You'll notice that there are many things left unsaid:

- A hefty list of apps for easy reference
- More resources about using the iPad
- Specific instructions on how apps work
- A description of YOUR favorite app (my apologies, I agree, there are blatant omissions)
- In-depth descriptions of all the available iPad accessories
- And more...

Well, if I give it all away here, you won't be tempted to check out my website. The book serves as an initial inspiration for what the iPad can do for your studio. My website offers

- The latest news about the iPad, the book simply cannot stay current as things change daily
- Reviews of the hippest apps
- A collection of opinions on the iPad and apps from others
- Encouragement for rookie iPad owners
- Advice from the pros (not necessarily me)
- In general, how to keep your revolutionary studio plugged into the power of apps.

Congratulations! With the purchase of this book you will now have access to the virtual support you've always dreamed of for understanding and using the iPad in your studio. Why then would I end this book with the quote below? That's a good question.

> *"You can't force yourself to submit to the tyranny of technology."*

A while back, Shana Kirk, Senior Editor of *Simpletec*, contacted me to provide some answers to questions for an article to be in the premiere edition of the magazine. She asked me what advice I would give to a teacher considering technology for the first time. Somehow, I came up with the quote above? I liked the sound of "tyranny of technology" so went with it. After completing all her questions in an email, I pushed the send button and moved on to the next task.

In the middle of the night I awoke with sudden clarity that I did NOT like that phrase and immediately revised my answer to the question and emailed it to Shana early the next morning. Apparently, it was too late to change and wouldn't you know, that phrase *"You can't force yourself to submit to the tyranny of technology"* was the pull line firmly planted in the middle of the page in large bold print.

Let's pause and review the definition of irony..."happening in the opposite way to what is expected and typically causing wry amusement because of this."

Yes, I was amused as I wondered how this statement might befuddle the readers. Why would someone who is considered forward thinking, as the magazine's column heading suggests, include such a quote in a publication devoted to teaching with technology? Although it was a little difficult to swallow, I began to embrace my harsh, almost negative statement in big black letters and decided that is was OK. OK, because it is true. No one should dive into technology if they are not ready for some pretty tough lessons and a steep learning curve.

 What does the thesaurus list for tyranny? Equivalents include enslavement, severity and ruthlessness.

Confession: I still find myself lost in a murky sea of questions - Why does Evernote not sync like it is supposed to? Why do pics in my Dropbox not appear where I thought they'd be? Why does this app crash all the time? Why can't I access the Internet here? Why does the idea of iCloud seem so foggy to me?

Despite it all, I challenge you to join the revolution and experience and grow from the "ruthlessness" of technology. Plug into the power of apps not just because of all the facts listed in the first chapter about today's high maintenance generation. Do it for you so that you continually build your skills as a creative teacher, musician and human being.

As Steve Jobs states:

"You can't connect the dots looking forward. You can only connect them looking backwards."

You may not make the connections right away but in time you will see the value of taking advantage of today's technology.

Jump on the technology bandwagon with both feet and hang on tight. There will be some bumps and potholes along the way so be prepared for a winding path. As my 89-year-old piano student who is also a proud iPad owner preaches: *build a bridge and get over it.*

THANK YOU

With any project of this magnitude there's countless people to thank. I'll start with the sole person who made this book become reality: my husband, Chuck. Besides being a faithful husband and best friend for over 26 years, he's been a fantastic father, incredible chef (I'm not exaggerating), taxi driver, grocery shopper, and patient supporter of all my technology woes and so much more.

Next in line would be my editors, Chuck Viss, Bradley Sowash, my mom, Joanne Alberda, and my son, Chase. They sacrificed hours reading through pages of documents to help me build chapters worthy of a book. Of course, my book designer, Ray Mong made the book come alive and for that I'm extremely grateful.

I would be remiss not to recognize Barbara Kreader, Michelle Sisler and Wendy Stevens for their ongoing support of my efforts and their kind words regarding this book.

And then there's Tom Folenta my co-publisher, marketer, managing editor, designer, advisor... We discovered all kinds of interesting things about each other as we carved a path to publishing this book. I'm not sure if I've met anyone who can fit quite as many words in one minute and knows as much about the world of marketing as Tom. I count myself extremely fortunate for joining creative forces with a friend and colleague like him and look forward to what the future holds as we plan to publish similar books supporting teachers like you in the world of technology.

The information in this book comes from years of exploring, experimenting and learning from others; so, a huge "thank you" to those who know more than me and who continue to inspire my efforts. One more "thank you" goes to you, the reader, for allowing me to share what I've gleaned with you.

-Leila

STAY CONNECTED • STAY INFORMED • STAY ON-TOP
TWO AMAZING PLACES – ONE DEDICATED MISSION

88PIANOKEYS.ME

It's not all black and white. There's more than one way to approach the art of teaching music and 88pianokeys.me is where you will find an assortment of resources, direction, practical suggestions, tools, inspiration, studio incentives, and encouragement. What you will find at the blog:

1) Music App Directory: lists apps organized into various categories for your convenience
2) Creative Corner: provides ideas for integrating creativity into every lesson
3) Online Book Club: hosts chats about favorite music-related books
4) Get Inspired! Series: features videos and information about music of various styles and hot artists
5) One App at a Time: includes reviews of the latest apps and how to incorporate them into daily teaching, and more...

Find 88pianokeys on Facebook, too!

MUSIC TEACHER TECHNOLOGY CAMPUS
WWW.MTTCAMPUS.COM

The iPad Piano Studio: Keys to Unlocking the Power of Apps is the first published title under a learning campaign focused on helping music educators succeed in today's digital world. At the heart of this spirited initiative, you will find our e-Team "insert TV theme here", plus a single-hub website location that houses it all –

• Technology books relevant to music educators
• Informative videos on digital communication
• Publishing services for teachers
  (books, ebooks, web)

• Website and mobile services
• Digital keyboard guides and the list goes on…

We call this exciting e-world, the "Music Teacher Technology Campus (MTTCampus.com), … we think you may call it digital nirvana – a place where you can feel at home even when understanding technology can make you feel like you're on the moon. If you need easy-to-understand direction and guidance so that you can move freely in today's digital world — and the comfort of knowing that you're not alone, our e-Team and even teachers just like you, are just a click away. We invite you to take the first step to digital enlightenment by becoming a member today.

Basic membership is free and the benefits are priceless. Simply visit www.MTTCampus.com and select the "Join Our Communi-Team" button.

DO YOU HAVE AN IPAD?
ARE YOU THINKING OF GETTING ONE?

This book provides the tools to help you tap into its full potential.

- Understand the benefits of using an iPad to enhance and improve your music studio
- Increase your productivity and save time and money
- Connect more efficiently with students of the mobile generation
- Learn about built-in apps, features, and accessories
- Discover a world of amazing apps and how to integrate them into your daily lesson instruction

Purchase includes these bonuses: a collection of associated videos, a Digital e-Book version and more.

What People are Saying...

"Congratulations! This is an excellent guide. I have read your outstanding book three different times now. I love your breezy yet factual style. The tone feels intimate; teachers will know you are "one of them." As you know, I am already a convert, but I learned a lot about making my own YouTube site and how to use Dropbox to better advantage!"
- Barbara Kreader, Keyboard Editor for Educational Publications at Hal Leonard Corporation,
  Contributing Editor of Clavier Companion

"Leila has written the most down to earth technology articles on both my and her blog. She makes technology doable for any teacher!"
- Wendy Stevens of ComposeCreate.com

"As an effective piano teacher who thinks outside the box, Leila takes you on a virtual trip into her iPad to show you how she creatively uses an iPad to enhance her teaching. Through this easy to read book, you can easily enhance your studio and have a variety of tools at your fingertips, available at a moment's notice whenever you need them."
- Michelle Sisler

LEILA VISS, AUTHOR

Leila is drawn to discovering innovative teaching methods to encourage the average player to stick to the bench for life. Customizing lessons for each student is a priority and therefore she provides "blended" instruction in Classical, Jazz, Pop along with creativity beyond the page.

Every student not only has a private lesson but a lab session as well. She is unashamedly infatuated with the iPad and the variety of apps and declares it has revolutionized her 21st-century teaching. The book is a direct result of her desire to share her new "love" with others.

$21.99
ISBN 978-0-9900010-0-3
52199>

9 780990 001003